Contemporary Orangeism in Canada

James W. McAuley · Paul Nesbitt-Larking

Contemporary Orangeism in Canada

Identity, Nationalism, and Religion

James W. McAuley
School of Human and Health Sciences
University of Huddersfield
Huddersfield, West Yorkshire
UK

Paul Nesbitt-Larking
Department of Political Science
Huron University College
London, ON
Canada

ISBN 978-3-319-61841-8   ISBN 978-3-319-61842-5 (eBook)
DOI 10.1007/978-3-319-61842-5

Library of Congress Control Number: 2017947716

© The Editor(s) (if applicable) and The Author(s) 2018
This work is subject to copyright. All rights are solely and exclusively licensed by the Publisher, whether the whole or part of the material is concerned, specifically the rights of translation, reprinting, reuse of illustrations, recitation, broadcasting, reproduction on microfilms or in any other physical way, and transmission or information storage and retrieval, electronic adaptation, computer software, or by similar or dissimilar methodology now known or hereafter developed.
The use of general descriptive names, registered names, trademarks, service marks, etc. in this publication does not imply, even in the absence of a specific statement, that such names are exempt from the relevant protective laws and regulations and therefore free for general use.
The publisher, the authors and the editors are safe to assume that the advice and information in this book are believed to be true and accurate at the date of publication. Neither the publisher nor the authors or the editors give a warranty, express or implied, with respect to the material contained herein or for any errors or omissions that may have been made. The publisher remains neutral with regard to jurisdictional claims in published maps and institutional affiliations.

Cover illustration: © Melisa Hasan

Printed on acid-free paper

This Palgrave Macmillan imprint is published by Springer Nature
The registered company is Springer International Publishing AG
The registered company address is: Gewerbestrasse 11, 6330 Cham, Switzerland

Preface

What does Orangeism look like in the diaspora, and what happens to Orange ideals and values as they move across oceans and through the decades and centuries? These are the core questions that motivated our research into the Orange Order in Canada. Our monograph, *Contemporary Orangeism in Canada*, is an exploration of the political identities and perspectives of the remaining members of a fraternal organization in decline. Once a highly influential organization embedded in the heart of Protestant English Canada, the Orange Order now depends upon the service, creativity, and commitment of a declining number of aging men. Based upon a series of in-depth interviews as well as content/discourse analyses, *Contemporary Orangeism in Canada* explores perspectives on religious faith, support for the Crown and the monarchy, attitudes toward the State, government, and public policy, and orientations toward community belonging. Among other focuses, our book considers the role of Protestantism in a secular and multicultural setting, attitudes toward immigration and integration, and responses to the recent expansion of socially liberal policies. *Contemporary Orangeism in Canada* will be of interest to students of Canadian society, members of fraternal organizations, members of the Orange Order, and students of religion and politics.

Huddersfield, UK James W. McAuley
London, Canada Paul Nesbitt-Larking

Acknowledgements

Our book brings together the voices of a small number of dedicated and loyal men, who continue to serve and support the Orange Order in Canada. Our research participants freely and generously gave of their time and their perspectives in a series of meaningful interviews. We were welcomed into homes and Orange halls, and we are most grateful for the kind hospitality of those Canadian Orangemen who volunteered to share some of their time with us.

While the research project on which this book is based received no formal funding, we are grateful to our educational institutions, the University of Huddersfield and Huron University College, for their ongoing support of our research. The Research Ethics Committee at Huron provided invaluable advice in the framing of our research questions and interview protocol. We thank Dr. Mark Cole, Chair of the Huron University College Research Ethics Committee, for his care and attention to detail throughout the approval process.

We are most grateful to our friend, Jo Trudgen, a descendant of Ontario Orangemen, who set up two interviews for us. We also wish to thank Allison Hibbert for her work in transcribing some of our interview material.

We also wish to express our profound gratitude to Stephanie Jameson and Carolyn Nesbitt-Larking, who supported us through this project and forgave us for the missing days spent on the road in southern Ontario.

Contents

1 Introduction   1

2 The Historical Setting   13

3 Faith   25

4 Crown   47

5 The State   63

6 Community   85

7 Conclusion   109

Appendix A   117

Appendix B   119

Appendix C: The Orange Order and Orangeism in Canada   121

Index   125

List of Figures

Fig. 2.1 Orange Lodges in Canada and Ontario 1890–2000 21
Fig. 6.1 The *Sentinel* 2007–2013—categories 95
Fig. 6.2 The *Sentinel* 2003–2013—sections 101

CHAPTER 1

Introduction

Abstract This chapter briefly sets the agenda for the study of the contemporary Orange Order and Orangeism in Canada and establishes a preliminary historical contextualization for the book, explaining its rise to prominence and its more recent post-war decline. A series of research questions, related to the continuity of Orangeism in the context of contemporary Canada, is briefly presented. Following this, a short description of each of the succeeding chapters is offered. This chapter continues with a brief presentation of three theoretical perspectives that inform the analyses: Social Identity Theory/Self-categorization Theory; memory and commemoration; and English Canadian exceptionalism. This chapter concludes with a brief description of methodologies undertaken to interview the research participants and to conduct content/discourse analyses of *The Sentinel*, the Canadian Orange journal.

Keywords Orange Order · Orangeism · Canada · Social Identity Theory · Commemoration

It is coming up to forty years since Houston and Smyth made the claim that Orangeism in Canada: "is a peripheral movement restricted to a minority of aging participants and incomprehensible to most observers" (Houston and Smyth 1980: 160). If Orangeism was peripheral in the late 1970s, today it has become almost invisible, and the aging participants are now older and even fewer in number. Why then have we turned our academic attention to a fraternal movement that now seems so marginal? Our research into what remains of the Orange Order in Canada serves two social scientific purposes that we find compelling. First, from a historical and structural perspective, throughout much of the nineteenth and twentieth centuries, the Orange Order had a dominant sociopolitical, religious, and economic presence in Canada. Historians have ably explained its decline in the context of Canadian developments (Houston and Smyth 1980; Wilson 2007; Smyth 2015), but none has examined the decline in the comparative framework of the fate of the Orange Order in Northern Ireland. How far do the trends that have influenced the decline in Canada reflect more general trends in Orangeism, and how far are the circumstances in the Canadian context unique? McAuley and his colleagues have examined in detail the contemporary Orange Order in Northern Ireland (McAuley 2010, 2016; McAuley et al. 2011). In this book, we examine the contemporary Orange Order in Canada in light of both that framework and contemporary Canadian sociopolitical life, which Nesbitt-Larking (2007, 2012, 2014), and Nesbitt-Larking and Bradford (2015) have investigated. In so doing, we reveal a series of fascinating comparisons and contrasts. We do this through our analyses of a range of primary and secondary documents, and in particular our content and discourse analysis of *The Sentinel*, the major publication of the Orange Order in Canada.

We also describe the reflections and responses of eighteen Canadian Orangemen, who generously devoted hours to conversations with us on contemporary Orangeism in Canada. Their information and insights furnished an invaluable resource as we attempted to address the experiential question of what it is like to be an Orangeman in contemporary Canada. It is their own words that inform the drive and direction of our book. This is the second major purpose of our research. Recent research on everyday resistance has uncovered the ways in which the marginalized and the oppressed are able to negotiate relations of power without access to conventional resources (de Certeau 1988; Scott 1990). How do women, ethno-racial and religious minorities, peasants, GBLTQ (gay, bisexual, lesbian, transgenered, queer) minorities, and others assert themselves and gain any influence in settings in which they are marginal and lack access to the dominant structures of power? Our work in this book builds upon certain insights derived from this scholarship, but applies them to the more mundane setting of a small community of aging white males in contemporary Canada. These are the members of the Orange Order. Our central purpose here is to explore the political realities of this once-dominant political and societal brotherhood, whose influence and status have undergone substantial diminution.

In the past, the Orange Order in Canada exerted substantial social and political influence, promoting the virtues of a united British Empire and the broad vision of a white Anglo-Saxon Protestant society. The central research challenge of our project is to investigate the continued relevance of the Orange Order (as an institutional and organizational presence) and Orangeism (as an ideology) in contemporary Canadian society. Historically, the presence of the Orange Order looms large. With its origins in the early nineteenth century, and its formal beginnings in Canada in 1830, the Orange Order is associated with loyalism and conservatism in such pivotal movements as the anti-rebellion forces of 1837 and the anti-Riel forces in the 1870s. Orangemen dominated Toronto politics in the first half of the twentieth century, and Sir John A. Macdonald and John Diefenbaker were just two of the prominent politicians who were Orangemen. Indeed, so dominant was the Order in Toronto from the mid-nineteenth to the mid-twentieth centuries that the city was referred to as "The Belfast of Canada" (Smyth 2015), both by its allies and its enemies. From its beginnings in the early nineteenth century, the Orange Order in Canada peaked in membership and influence in the 1920s. In 1921, the population of Canada was just under 8,800,000. At that time, the Orange Order consisted of at least 100,000 members (a conservative estimate), with many more who had been through an Orange Lodge or were related to a member (Wilson 2007: 21). In 1980, Houston and Smyth reported: "fewer than twenty thousand active members in the country and their average age cannot be less than fifty years" (Houston and Smyth 1980: 167). By June 2013, there were only 2,536 men (personal communication) remaining in the Orange Order across Canada in a population of 35,154,300. While the numbers do not tell the entire story, there is no denying the fact that contemporary Orangeism in Canada has been in serious decline since the 1950s (Smyth 2015). Throughout our interviews and examinations of contemporary Orange Order documents, we detect a sense of dignity and hope combined with a realistic appraisal of where Orangeism stands in Canada today. There is a certain poignancy about the decline in the ranks of Canadian Orangemen, evidenced in the words of Ontario West Grand Master, Dennis Glazier in 2011, who wrote:

> The past year for this executive has been challenging to say the least. This in no way should be considered negative as we were up for each and every opportunity and welcomed them all ... Our mission is to promote the Orange Order and do whatever possible to continue the operation in many communities; however, we must be realistic. If the ownership of a building is crippling a lodge and their membership is not evolving for tomorrow, the lodge has to consider redevelopment by amalgamation or selling the property. On a sad point, the year has again fallen witness to departed brothers which [sic] the Grand Secretary will give tribute. (Grand Orange Lodge of Ontario West 2011: 10, 12)

The Report of the Grand Secretary of Ontario West for 2011 indicates that only around thirty men became new members in the previous year, while at least seventeen were recorded as having passed away (Grand Orange Lodge of Ontario West 2011: 17, 18). While the year in review confronted the Association with the serious challenge of locating sufficient qualified men to fill various ceremonial offices, the spirit of pride and loyalty remained in place.

Our book is a detailed analysis of the ideas and ideals of those men who have kept the faith and who continue to meet, to organize, and to promote their Orange principles, increasingly now cut off both from Northern Irish roots and their own Canadian heritage. Throughout the book, we attempt to describe and analyze these perspectives with honesty, respect, and a critical orientation. The sociodemographic and structural insertion into contemporary Canadian society makes it inaccurate to describe them as marginal and as an oppressed minority. Being white, Protestant, and male carries with it a range of structured and historically conditioned privileges. These are further sustained by the adherence of most members of the Orange Order to a highly conventional and conservative belief system. It is, however, also inaccurate to describe contemporary Canadian Orangemen as members of a dominant elite. Throughout their history and even when they held a great deal of influence, they were outsiders to the establishment and excluded from the ruling classes. While their loyalty might have served a useful purpose in legitimizing the imperial order, their tribalism and literalism rendered them too crude and rough-hewn for the arenas of political and diplomatic life. In contemporary Canada, lacking now in numbers, social status, and influence, they share in common with the oppressed an invisibility and, if they are recognized at all, the popular portrayal of their core beliefs in stereotypical and negative ways that they are decreasingly able to correct in the court of public opinion. And yet, a few of them carries on and the Orange Order survives. If they cannot be said to practice everyday *resistance*, they are certainly practitioners of everyday *resilience*.

Among the most compelling reminders of this is the annual Toronto Orange Parade. The longest-running continuous Orange parade in North America, it is now coming up to its 200th year. In the heyday of the Canadian Orange Order, there would have been thousands marching and tens of thousands out to cheer along the thronged sidewalks. In recent years, with great effort, the Orange Order has been able to gather a few hundred marchers. However, their audience has dwindled to a few pockets of bemused bystanders, who while not hostile are only fitfully curious. What is it that compels the fidelity of these men in an era which in so many ways runs counter to their beliefs and interests? What are their hopes and their lamentations? How do they manifest their pride? How far do they recognize and support those emergent political projects of nation and tradition that might be regarded as relatively compatible with their belief systems? Do they regard them as a lifeline?

The reactionary return to a more assertive British Canadianism (Buckner 2005; Champion 2010), promoted by the recently defeated Conservative government as part of a strategy to undermine the legacy of post-war Liberal Canada, offered some support to the principles that Canadian Orangemen have traditionally espoused. How far did this opportunity in political cultural leadership resonate with the Orangemen? Did they enthusiastically endorse the Harper Conservative Party's royalist agenda? Who do they regard as allies and as adversaries? How do they contend with the "hidden injuries of class" (Sennett and Cobb 1973), and what they perceive to be an ungrateful political community? In general, how do they manifest their political beliefs? Given the decline in their membership, how far do they adhere to the orthodoxies and narratives of "faith, crown and state" (McAuley and Tonge 2007, 2008), and how far have they attempted to adapt and modify in order to rebuild? In order to address these and related questions, we conducted extensive semi-structured interviews with eighteen mostly older Orangemen in Southern Ontario from 2012 to 2014. We also undertook a content and discourse analysis of *The Sentinel*, the official publication of the Canadian Orange Order.

To anticipate the general direction of our findings, our Orange Order interviewees displayed a sense of anchoring and pride in their Protestant heritage, loyalty to the Crown and a comfort at being a part of a British

Canadian heritage. The context for McAuley and Tonge's (2007, 2008) analysis is the recent politics of Northern Ireland. While the Orange Order in Canada has recruited from the Ulster diaspora and retains strong fraternal bonds, it has always lacked the structural divisions and negative interdependencies that condition sectarian politics in Northern Ireland. To begin with, divisions in housing and neighborhoods never developed in Canada, where Catholics and Protestants have routinely coexisted as neighbors (Houston and Smith 1980: 109). Such distinctions assist us in conceptualizing the character of Orangeism in contemporary Canada. The distinctions between Northern Ireland and Canada are clear to Northern Irish Orange leader and historian David Hume, who in a recent article notes the tone of Protestant–Catholic relations in Toronto:

> I am mindful of an example from Toronto early in the 20th century of how an Orange parade was rerouted around the home of a prominent Roman Catholic who was extremely ill. This man had put up an Orange flag at his home each Twelfth. The two gestures were deeply symbolic: they show us that it is possible to have mutual respect and tolerance while still practicing our own heritage and culture. (Hume 2012)

As we shall see, when it comes to both the geopolitical and spatial character of loyalism and the identity strategies surrounding Protestantism, there are important and systematic distinctions between Orangeism in Canada and Northern Ireland. We have organized our account of the principal views of Canadian Orangemen into five subsequent chapters: The Historical Setting, Faith, Crown, State, and Community.

Chapter 2, The Historical Setting, sets out a brief historical contextualization to the lives of contemporary Canadian Orangemen. We make no attempt to offer a complete historical account and defer to those historians who have already conducted research into the Orange Order in Canada (Senior 1972; Houston and Smyth 1980, 2007; Thomson 1983; Pennefather 1984; Kealey 1995; Radforth 2004, 2007; Clarke 2007; Jenkins 2007; Kaufmann 2007; MacRaild 2007; Wilson 2007; Smyth 2015). The selective account of strands of Orange history serves to situate and contextualize the findings in the subsequent chapters and to give a coherent account of the principal dynamics informing Orangeism in contemporary Canada.

Chapter 3 is an exploration of the core faith of contemporary Orangemen in Canada. What does their Protestantism mean to them?

How do they practice their beliefs? How far do they consider themselves to be Christians? How do they relate to Catholics and Catholicism? What understandings do they have of other religions, notably Islam?

In Chap. 4, we present views and perspectives on the Crown. This includes values and beliefs surrounding the monarchy, both as a cultural symbol and as a constitutional principle. Chapter 4 also explores the relationship between the Crown and Canada's military presence, a focus that has been recently accentuated through the royalist projects of the Harper Conservative Party.

The State is the focus of Chap. 5. Here, we undertake an analysis of the views of contemporary Canadian Orangemen on the Constitution, government, governance, political life, and a range of public policy issues. This includes immigration, the French fact in Canada and bilingualism, and sexual politics.

In the final substantive chapter, Chap.6, we define and examine orientations toward the community. Also included in Chap. 6 are accounts of the views of contemporary Canadian Orangemen on gender, in-group solidarity, community outreach, parades and marching, social and cultural capital, and the politics of respectability.

THEORETICAL AND METHODOLOGICAL NOTES

Our analyses throughout the book are informed by at least three compatible theoretical traditions: first, the broad traditions of Social Identity Theory and Self-categorization Theory in political and social psychology (Sindic and Condor 2014). These traditions examine how people come to self-categorize and to categorize others as members of certain groups, how they develop identifications, and under what circumstances they draw comparisons and contrasts among various groups. This theoretical perspective on identities regards them as dynamic and relational and subject to change through time and space. Moreover, identities may be formed strategically in relations of power, and as such, they are in competition, contested, and may be conflicting. The inclusion of certain others as members of the in-group, or the out-group, will vary according to time and context, as will exclusion of those deemed to be members of the out-group.

Second, and related to this, memory is a contested field, and those who invoke memory in the service of identity claims do so on the basis of imagined identities (Assmann 2005; Halbwachs 1992; Olick 2007).

As with all members of fraternal organizations, Orange members draw upon selective memories as a core aspect of this construction of identity. In so doing, they prioritize and mythologize parts of the past through the selective and partial use of chosen traumas and chosen glories (Volkan 2001). In constructing their pasts, contemporary Canadian Orangemen are necessarily selective in their memory work and invoke traditions and rituals that are an amalgam of original and borrowed materials. Those that are borrowed are predominantly rooted in Northern Ireland, thereby forging bonds of collective memory and cultural tradition across the Atlantic.

The third theoretical tradition is that of the distinctiveness of Canadian political culture as a setting for the evolution of contemporary Orangeism. Bringing together elements of the ideologies of traditional conservatism, socialism, and liberalism, the creation of a multicultural and civic nationalist polity throughout English Canada has served as a basis for explaining political life in contemporary Canada, including the broad acceptance of ethno-cultural and religious diversity, and support for multiculturalism, notwithstanding continued problems of coloniality, systemic racism, and discrimination (Nesbitt-Larking 2012; Nesbitt-Larking and McAuley forthcoming; Wiseman 2007). Such an embedded political culture has conditioned the growth and development of Canadian Orangeism in a distinctive manner, and the consequences of such conditioning are evident in the expressed values and ideas of our research participants.

From 2012 to 2014, we welcomed the oppotunity to converse with, and in some cases, enjoyed the hospitality of Orange members whilst we conducted 18 in-depth semi-structured interviews with Orangemen in South-Western Ontario and the Toronto area. These interviews were conducted following approval of an interview protocol and questions through the Huron University College Research Ethics Committee. Those interviewed included both those in leadership positions as well as ordinary members. Establishing contact and building trust were challenging, and the process of identifying people, times, and places to meet and talk included many false starts, failed attempts, and multiple communications. On first meeting, some participants explained to us that previous encounters with researchers and journalists had generated publications that attacked, misrepresented, or belittled the Orange Order, and that they were, therefore, somewhat reticent to participate. Our pledge to them was to assume their personal integrity, to respect them and their commitment, and to engage in analytical academic analysis. We further guaranteed that their words would be treated in confidence. Throughout this book, we make use of pseudonyms. We stated that we would present a critical account of their truths, but in so doing would strive to be fair, describing the reality of Orangeism, Orangemen, and the Orange Order in contemporary Canada with sincerity, objectivity, and balance. We enjoyed the opportunity to converse with, and in some cases, the home hospitality of, a small number of mostly senior men who generously opened up their worlds to us. These men are the remaining stalwarts of an organization in numerical and organizational decline, with fewer members and lodges in each successive year. In their own view, the future of the Orange Order is uncertain at best, even as some of them find small grounds for optimism. What is clear above all is their loyal commitment, their deep comradeship, and their continued hard work on behalf of the Orange Order.

The standard bearer for Orange news and views in Canada for over a century has been *The Sentinel*. While its first two years of publication were patchy, *The Sentinel* became an influential and respected weekly paper from 1875 until 2002 (Thomson 1983). Like *The Orange Standard* in Northern Ireland, *The Sentinel* was for decades a proud banner of Orange views and a chronicle of the Orange Order: "…for more than a century it had been a popular organ for thousands of Orangemen, propagating a certain sense of politics and history and inculcating a view of self-perceived importance" (Houston and Smyth 2007: 189). Facing declining enrolment and interest, the paper has since 2002 become an in-house journal published three times per year. The only continuing viable source for its funding is the modest profits of Orange Insurance, which also funds a range of other core Orange activities across Canada. Funding by Orange Insurance may be a factor in the centralized, bland, and rather bureaucratic tone that seems to characterize the magazine. As early as 1980, there were reports of: "growing lists of death notices published in the Sentinel…" (Houston and Smyth 1980: 167). In addition to material on the convivial aspects of life in the Orange Order, this remains the predominant tone and style of *The Sentinel* today.

Our content and discourse analysis of ten years of the journal (2003–2013) is based upon 28 of the 35 published issues, an 80% sample. Our methodology of discourse analysis follows the work of Potter and Wetherell (1987). Potter and Wetherell point out that discourses are *actions* as well as symbolic expressions. As ideologically constituted entities, discourses privilege certain readings of the world and prefer certain interpretations. Discourses identify an existential world (what exists); a moral code (what is good and what is evil), and—most powerfully, and least obviously—an epistemological order (what is possible and what is impossible). Discourses work in the construction of reality and experience in concrete and material ways. Discourses are the ideal site at which to unearth the work of ideology in shaping and privileging aspects of the broader culture through the subjective and intersubjective work of reception. As Billig says: "...ideology operates through the mobilization of discourse. Thus, the processes of ideology, as means of mobilizing meaning, are also means of mobilizing consciousnesses" (1991: 14). How then is the imagined world of Canadian Orangemen over the past five years constructed? What partial readings of the world does it privilege and promote? How does it aim to mobilize Orangemen to further agency? These are the questions that we examine in the substantive chapters, notably in Chap. 6 on Community. Overall, the book goes some way to describing the worldview of members of the Orange Order in Canada; their understanding of the social world in which they find themselves; and their ideological and political responses to it. We turn next in Chap. 2 to an historical contextualization of the Orange Order and Orangeism in Canada.

REFERENCES

Assmann, Jan. *Religion and Cultural Memory: Ten Studies*. Stanford: Stanford University Press, 2005.
Billig, Michael. *Ideology and Opinions: Studies in Rhetorical Psychology*. London: Sage, 1991.
Buckner, Phillip. "Introduction." In *Canada and the End of Empire*, edited by Phillip Buckner, 1–14. Vancouver: University of British Columbia Press, 2005.
Champion, C.P. *The Strange Demise of British Canada: The Liberals and Canadian Nationalism, 1964–1968*. Kingston: McGill-Queen's University Press, 2010.
Clarke, B. "Religious Riot as Pastime: Orange Young Britons, Parades and Public Life in Victorian Toronto." In *The Orange Order in Canada*, edited by D.A. Wilson, 109–127. Dublin: Four Courts Press, 2007.
de Certeau, Michel. *The Practice of Everyday Life*. Berkeley: University of California Press, 1988.
Grand Orange Lodge of Ontario West. *Report of Proceedings of the 152nd Annual Sessions of the Right Worshipful Provincial Grand Lodge of Ontario West*. Niagara Falls. April 28–30th 2011. Unpublished.

Halbwachs, Maurice. *On Collective Memory*. Chicago: University of Chicago Press, 1992.

Houston, Cecil J. & William J. Smyth. *The Sash Canada Wore: A Historical Geography of the Orange Order in Canada*. Toronto: University of Toronto Press, 1980.

Houston, Cecil J & Smyth, William J. "The Faded Sash: The Decline of the Orange Order in Canada, 1920–2005." in *The Orange Order in Canada*, edited by D.A. Wilson, 170–192. Four Courts Press: Dublin, 2007.

Hume, David. "It's Colours They Are Fine—All Over the World." *The Belfast Telegraph*, Friday July 13, 2012. http://www.belfasttelegraph.co.uk/opinion/news-analysis/its-colours-they-are-fine-all-overAccessed April 15, 2016.

Jenkins, William. "View From 'the Hub of the Empire': Loyal Orange Lodges in Early Twentieth-century Toronto." In *The Orange Order in Canada*, edited by D.A. Wilson, 128–145. Dublin: Four Courts Press, 2007.

Kaufmann, Eric. "The Orange Order in Ontario, Newfoundland, Scotland and Northern Ireland: A Macro-social Analysis." In *The Orange Order in Canada*, edited by D.A. Wilson, 42–68. Dublin: Four Courts Press, 2007.

Kealey, Gregory. "Orangemen and the Corporation: The Politics of Class in Toronto During the Union of the Canadas." In *Workers and Canadian History*, edited by Gregory Kealey, 163–208. Kingston: McGill-Queen's University Press, 1995.

MacRaild, Donald M. "The Associationalism of the Orange Diaspora." In *The Orange Order in Canada*, edited by D.A. Wilson, 25–41. Dublin: Four Courts Press, 2007.

McAuley, James W. *Ulster's Last Stand? (Re)Constructing Ulster Unionism After the Peace Process*. Dublin: Irish Academic Press, 2010.

McAuley, James W. *Very British Rebels? The Culture and Politics of Ulster Loyalism*. New York: Bloomsbury, 2016.

McAuley, James W. & Jon Tonge. ""For God and for the Crown": Contemporary Political and Social Attitudes among Orange Order Members in Northern Ireland." *Political Psychology* 28.1. (2007): 33–52.

McAuley, James W. & Jon Tonge. ""Faith, Crown and State": Contemporary Discourses within the Orange Order in Northern Ireland." *Peace and Conflict Studies* 15.1. (2008): 136–155.

McAuley, James W., Jon Tonge & Andrew Mycock. *Loyal to the Core? Contemporary Orangeism and Politics in Northern Ireland*. Dublin: Irish Academic Press, 2011.

Nesbitt-Larking, Paul. *Politics, Society and the Media*. Toronto: University of Toronto Press, 2007.

Nesbitt-Larking, Paul. "Canadian Political Culture: The Problem of Americanization." In *Crosscurrents*. 7th edition. Edited by P. Barker and M. Charlton, 4–22. Toronto: Nelson, 2012.

Nesbitt-Larking, Paul. "The Politics of Public Opinion." In *Publicity and the Canadian State: Critical Communications Approaches*, edited by Kirsten Kozolanka, 113–131. Toronto: University of Toronto Press, 2014.

Nesbitt-Larking, Paul & Neil Bradford. "The 'Good Enough' Multicultural City: Managing Diversity in Toronto." In *Divided Cities: Governing Contested Issues*, edited by Annika Björkdahl and Lisa Strömbom, 37–57. Nordic Academic Press / Svenska historiska media AB, 2015.

Nesbitt-Larking, Paul & James W. McAuley. "Securitization through Re-Enchantment: The Strategic Uses of Myth and Memory." *Postcolonial Studies*. Forthcoming.

Olick, Jeffrey K. *The Politics of Regret: On Collective Memory and Historical Responsibility*. London: Routledge, 2007.

Pennefather, R.S. *The Orange and the Black: Documents in the History of the Orange Order Ontario and the West, 1890–1940*. Canada: Orange and Black Publications, 1984.

Potter, Jonathan & Margaret Wetherell. *Discourse and Social Psychology: Beyond Attitudes and Behaviour*. London: Sage, 1987.

Radforth, Ian. *Royal Spectacle: The 1860 Visit of the Prince of Wales to Canada and the United States*. Toronto: University of Toronto Press, 2004.

Radforth, Ian. "Orangemen and the Crown." In *The Orange Order in Canada*, edited by D.A. Wilson, 69–88. Dublin: Four Courts Press, 2007.

Scott, J.C. *Domination and the Arts of Resistance: Hidden Transcripts*. New Haven: Yale University Press, 1990.

Senior, Hereward. *Orangeism: The Canadian Phase*. Toronto: McGraw-Hill Ryerson, 1972.

Sennett, Richard & Jonathan Cobb. *The Hidden Injuries of Class*. New York: Knopf, 1973.

Sindic, Denis & Susan Condor, "Social Identity Theory and Self-Categorization Theory." In *The Palgrave Handbook of Global Political Psychology*, edited by Paul Nesbitt-Larking, Catarina Kinnvall and Tereza Capelos, pp.39–54 London: Palgrave Macmillan, 2014.

Smyth, William J. *Toronto, the Belfast of Canada: The Orange Order and the Shaping of Municipal Culture*. Toronto: University of Toronto Press, 2015.

Thomson, A. (1983). *The Sentinel and Orange and Protestant Advocate, 1877–1896: An Orange view of Canada*. Theses and Dissertations (Comprehensive). Paper 10. Submitted in partial fulfilment of M.A. degree, Wilfrid Laurier University. http://scholars.wlu.ca/etd/10.

Volkan, Vamik. "Psychoanalysis and Diplomacy: Part 1. Individual and Large Group Identity." *Journal of Applied Psychoanalytic Studies* 1.1. (2001): 29–55.

Wilson, D.A. "Introduction." In *The Orange Order in Canada*, edited by D.A. Wilson, Dublin: Four Courts Press, 2007, 9–24.

Wiseman, Nelson. *In Search of Canadian Political Culture*. Vancouver: University of Vancouver Press, 2007.

CHAPTER 2

The Historical Setting

Abstract This chapter sets out a brief historical contextualization to the lives of contemporary Canadian Orangemen. The selective account of strands of Orange history serves to situate and contextualize the findings in the subsequent chapters and to give a coherent account of the principal dynamics informing Orangeism in contemporary Canada. This chapter begins with an account of early Orange immigration in Canada and conflicts with the Americans, the French, and the Roman Catholics. This chapter continues with a description of the cultural, political, economic, and religious development of Orangeism in the nineteenth and early twentieth centuries. This chapter concludes with an analysis of the postwar decline of Orangeism, based upon the growth of English Canadian nationalism, ethnic diversity, secularism, and the Welfare State.

Keywords Orangemen · Canadian history · French Canada Nationalism · Secularism

While our empirical evidence reveals an abiding spirit of determination, faith, and hope among contemporary Canadian Orangemen, it is clearly a fraternal organization in decline. In 2007, Houston and Smyth said: "(t)o describe the Orange Order as a faded and largely irrelevant organization in Canada in 2005 is to state the obvious" (2007: 170). Despite their will and commitment, those that remain members of the rapidly declining number of lodges are often inactive through the incapacitation and weariness of aging. In many cases, there are simply too few members remaining to conduct the tasks of running the societies. While there are new members each year, that number too is dwindling as the perceived relevance and influence of the Canadian Orange Order fades. The numerical and organizational decline of the Orange Order stands in stark contrast to its legacy as among the most important community organizations in English Canadian history. Historians are rightly focussed on the numerical power and pervasiveness of the Orange Order in Canada of the late nineteenth and early twentieth centuries. As we have stated, at its peak in the early twentieth century, the Orange Order was a prominent and powerful public presence. Its 1920 Toronto July parade attracted over 8000 marchers along with 20,000–25,000 onlookers and supporters (Smyth 2015: 212–213; Wilson 2007: 10). Local government and patronage were so tightly controlled by the Orange Order in the nineteenth- and early twentieth-century Toronto that it was often an occupational or social necessity to be from an Orange family in order to acquire a position or achieve a certain status (Kaufmann 2007: 62; Houston and Smyth 2007: 173). Historically, Protestantism, the Crown, and loyalty to Britain were critical in the context of an emerging English Canada of the early to mid-nineteenth century. From being a linguistic minority in the early nineteenth century, through immigration, anglophones grew to become the majority population by the 1850s. In this regard, they emerged as a dominant, but an anxious minority, facing a range of simultaneous threats. To begin with, there was an omnipresent threat from the Americans south of the border. The USA had declared independence from Britain following a revolutionary war. What is today known as Canada remained as a series of thinly populated colonies, referred to collectively as British North America.

The presence of the American republic was experienced simultaneously as a threat and an opportunity. The threat was the almost constant risk of invasion from the South and the hostile takeover of British North America. This threat broke out into a series of skirmishes and small battles in the War of 1812. The opportunity was the ever-present seductive pull of liberty and independence that was contained in Article XI of the Articles of Confederation that had specifically invited Canada to become an American state. Canadian political history throughout the nineteenth century is in large part a struggle between the conservative loyalism of the British connection and the liberal radicalism that came with sharing a continent with the USA and its promise of freedom from colonial tyranny.

Protestant Canadians within anglophone Canada faced other perceived threats, notably the numerically dominant French concentrated mostly to the East of the Ottawa River and the Irish Catholics of both Lower Canada (today's Quebec) and Upper Canada (today's Ontario). Given the internal and external ethno-political characteristics of post-Conquest Canada, Orangeism made sense. Both the Crown and the Protestant faith were under threat from forces both outside of and within the emerging British North American colonies.

As the USA went through its revolutionary break with Britain and the Crown, the imperial bonds of British North America became ever more relevant throughout the late eighteenth and nineteenth centuries. The bond to the British Crown grew stronger through the War of 1812 and the settlement of thousands of United Empire Loyalists, who had fled the USA following the revolution. From within Canada, the French, combined with the growing presence of Irish Catholic immigrants, posed a constant threat to Protestant hegemony (Senior 1972: 7). The Orange Order regarded and presented itself as a bulwark against the tides of Catholicism that consistently threatened to wash over Protestant Canada.

While the French in the Canadas had been conquered in the battle of the Plains of Abraham in 1759, the original settlers, referred to as "les habitants," remained a numerically dominant population until well into the nineteenth century. Encouraged by their priests, who occupied elite roles in French Canadian society, the French settlers produced large families. While they had been conquered militarily, this largely peasant society could exact what came to be known as "la revanche des berceaux," or the revenge of the cradle. This was the basis of French Canadian nationalism throughout the nineteenth and early twentieth centuries. The anglophone elite alternated in its response between assimilation and accommodation, and the consequent struggles between French and English communities were protracted and often violent. Writing on the rebellions against the elites in Upper and Lower Canada in 1838, Lord Durham famously described the French and English in Canada as "two nations warring within the bosom of a single state" (Durham 1982).

While the majority of Irish immigrants to Canada in the early nineteenth century were Protestants, certainly up to the 1830s (Toner and Leitch 2016), there was an influx of Catholic Irish following the decades of the Irish potato famine in the 1840s and 1850s. The conflict between the Protestant and Catholic Irish diasporas flared up at various times, notably around the assassination of the Canadian anti-Fenian Father of

Confederation, Thomas D'Arcy McGee in 1868 (Wilson 2015) and the execution of Orangeman Thomas Scott under the orders of rebel leader Louis Riel in 1870 (Bumstead 2015). Smyth notes:

> Orange leaders managed to link the ambitions of their organization with a projected Canadian national identity. Active in defeating Mackenzie's 1837 Rebellion, Orangemen claimed prominence in resisting the Fenian invasions of Canada in the decade of Confederation, and took especial pride in thwarting the Riel Rebellions in the Canadian West, avenging in the process the death of Thomas Scott, himself a lifelong Orangeman. Such national political crises, in combination with a long-standing suspicion of French and Catholic populations in Quebec, helped sustain an Orange garrison mentality. (Smyth 2015: 5)

Following its establishment in Co. Armagh, Ireland, in 1795, the Orange Order spread to the Canadas within a few years. Already by 1800, there were Orange Lodges in Halifax and Montreal (Houston and Smyth 2007: 171). In 1830, Ogle Gowan, recognized as the father of Canadian Orangeism, founded the Grand Lodge of British America in Brockville, Ontario. Between 1825 and 1845, over 250,000 Protestant Irish immigrants arrived and settled in the Canadas and in Ontario, and two out of three Irish immigrants in those decades were Protestants (Houston and Smyth 2007: 171). The Orange Order was to become the heart of the cultural and political fabric of Canada, notably Newfoundland, New Brunswick, and Ontario, throughout the nineteenth and well into the twentieth centuries. Wilson notes that: "the Orange Order functioned both as an ideological political organization, and as a religious fraternal organization with deep communal roots" (2007: 14).

Such characteristics help to explain both the longevity and the success of Orangeism in Canada. For Houston and Smyth, the "Orange Order, with its strident monarchical Britishness, defensive Protestantism and resolute anti-Catholicism, exhibits a fusion of political and religious beliefs that is fundamentally eighteenth century in construction" (2007: 170). MacRaild describes Orangeism as "a mixture of different aspects: social club, pseudo-religious sect, benefit society and militant political movement" (MacRaild 2007: 26). For thousands of working-class Protestants arriving in the Canadas of the nineteenth century, the existence of a robust and dependable mutual and fraternal society was more than merely a club; it quickly became a deeply integral aspect of social, cultural, and economic well-being for the man, his family, and community.

The Orange Order was a sanctuary for ethno-religious solidarity, mutual support, and conviviality. By the time of Confederation, the Orange Order was at the center of community life across Canada. Senior notes that:

> By 1867 Orangemen had found a secure place in Canadian society. There were few villages or urban neighbourhoods without an Orange hall. With its insurance fund, its youth section and its substantial press, the Orange movement had evolved into one of the most powerful popular organizations in the new Dominion. (1972: 95)

Clarke (2007: 112–113) identifies three dominant themes that characterized the speeches of Orange orators around July 12th parades: first, the idealization of Protestantism and the derogation of Catholicism; second, celebration of the imperial connection to Britain; and third, a determination to defend and fight for the Protestant faith and the British Empire. It also had great significance as a mutual society and benevolent society in a material sense, sustaining and supporting the Protestant faith and their families in the anti-combination and pre-welfare state decades. Within the context of the glories of the British Empire in the late nineteenth and early twentieth centuries, the Orange Order channeled the ethos of muscular Christianity and the exuberant celebration of imperial duty, fidelity, and heroism through the large-scale organized sports, musical, and leisure activities that were popular (Campbell 2010). Referring to the Toronto lodges of the early twentieth century, Jenkins says: "Fraternalism, loyalty and masculinity intersected in these Protestant spaces, complementing more fanciful ideas about adventure and heroism that these young men had imbibed during their school years" (Jenkins 2007: 130).

While the cultural, political, and religious origins of the Orange Order in Canada are of undoubted importance, our analysis should not overlook the profound materialism behind the growth and coming to dominance of the Orange Order in Canada throughout the nineteenth and early twentieth centuries. The Order was overwhelmingly a working-class organization and was associated from the start with both labor unions and benevolent societies. The Orange Order acted to sustain and support the Protestant faith and their families in the anti-combination and pre-welfare state decades. Most importantly, the Orange Order established an insurance branch, the Orange Mutual Benefit Fund, in 1881 that in the words of Smyth: "operated on the principles of contemporary actuarial science" (Smyth 2015: 91).

In the City of Toronto, the Orange Order monopolized jobs in the police and fire services throughout the late nineteenth and early twentieth centuries (Smyth 2015: 136). The most successful of the early editors of the Orange newspaper, *The Sentinel*, was Edward Frederick Clarke, a leading labor activist and militant (Thomson 1983; Kealey 1995). Just as in Britain under Disraeli, the post-Confederation Canada of Sir John A. Macdonald reinvented Conservatism to encompass organized labor, placing the emphasis on affective bonds of social and community solidarity and thereby undermining the radical and liberal agenda.

While the Canadian Orange Order was split throughout the nineteenth century, it increasingly came to associate itself with the Conservative Party. The Orange Order was profoundly integrated into civic and public life, with many elected and unelected Orange officials achieving success, notably in Toronto. Throughout the late nineteenth century and the first half of the twentieth century, the Orange Order came to dominate City Hall and the ranks of elected officialdom in Toronto. With reference to the years 1900–1940, Smyth comments: "Nowhere outside of the Ulster metropolis did the Orange Order maintain such a tight grip on public and private employment" (Smyth 2015: 209). In 1923, 41 out of the 75 elected Conservative Ontario provincial MPPs under Premier G. Howard Ferguson were Orangemen (Smyth 2015: 212). The Orange Order exerted a great deal of political influence in post-Confederation Canada, not just at the municipal level (few non-Orangemen were mayors of Toronto until the 1960s) but also at the provincial and federal levels (four Conservative premiers of Ontario were Orangemen and four Conservative prime ministers were Orangemen, including Sir John A. Macdonald). Irrespective of the shifting political allegiances of the nineteenth century, by the twentieth century, the Orange movement was solidly Conservative in Ontario and Canada, if not in Newfoundland.

Anti-Catholicism was foundational to the Orange Order and with it came a generalized opposition to French Canada. Disparaging parallels were frequently drawn between French and Irish Catholics, both communities regarded as feckless, disloyal, and a threat to Protestant values and property. And yet from the start, the anti-Catholic message was qualified and nuanced. From the nineteenth century, the complexities of Canadian brokerage politics have consistently favored cross-cutting cleavages in which regions, religions, and languages are brought together through elite accommodation in order to craft winning coalitions that can govern at a national level on the basis of adequate pockets of support. In a manner that might be inconceivable to outside observers, Kaufmann makes reference to the: "'Orange-Green-Bleu' post-1836 alliance which united Irish and French Catholics with Ontario Orange Protestants" (2007: 64).

Such a coalition brought together those of a conservative and loyalist tendency who were fighting against the anti-establishment and pro-American liberal and secularizing forces of reform. According to Kealey (1995: 186–187), the father of Canadian Orangeism, Ogle Gowan, adopted a pragmatic and moderate approach on the Catholic question and supported the alliance with the Quebec ultramontane "bleus," favoring thereby an alliance of those promoting the imperial connection, social respectability, and the Canadian establishment.

Politically, this paralleled the project of Sir John A. Macdonald and Sir George-Etienne Cartier, who founded the modern Canadian Conservative Party. Against Gowan were those Canadian Orangemen who adopted a strict anti-Catholic and pro-American nativism that also thereby set itself at odds with the British state and the politics of elite accommodation (See also Senior 1972: 21). In the broader context of Canadian history, the Orange Order always faced contradictions, given the more general necessity for compromise, accommodation, and balance in bringing elements of the political society together. In such a setting, an unvarnished Protestant loyalism, along with demands for rigid uniformity, unilingualism, monologism, and monoculturalism, could not survive. In this context, it is understandable that, according to Thomson, the anti-Catholic tone of *The Sentinel* was: "in some instances surprisingly temperate and less strident than historians have hitherto believed" (Thomson 1983: 1).

Pennefather points out that: "In Ireland the Order was by-and-large an instrument of the establishment. In Canada, the Order had significant disagreements with representatives of the establishment. This was applicable to both Conservative and Liberal-oriented establishments" (Pennefather 1984: 3). Thus, while as Protestants, Canadian Orangemen railed against the Conservative elite compromises that extended the rights of Catholics and francophones, as monarchists and loyalists, they also opposed Liberal moves toward Free Trade and the Americanization of Canada. (In)famously, on the occasion of the Royal visit of the Prince of Wales in 1860, members of the Orange Order, who had been forbidden to display colors and banners in conformity with British legislation, defiantly disobeyed the command in what can be described as a disloyal act of loyalism. At one point on the Prince's drive through Toronto on September 7, 1860, some Orangemen even attempted to drag his horse and carriage through a decorated Orange arch (Radforth 2004).

It is on the basis of these pragmatic considerations, conditioned by a range of temporal and spatial circumstances, that underscores Gregory Kealey's point that while the ideology of Crown, empire, and the Protestant faith have been abiding principles of Orangeism, it has: "had to be constantly reformulated in the Canadian context" (1995: 163). This profound insight assists us in understanding both the historical and contemporary place of Orangeism in Canada. As we argue throughout the book, accommodations and alliances have necessitated a broad and encompassing pragmatism on the part of Orangeism in Canada that continues to the present day.

From its beginnings in the early nineteenth century, the Orange Order in Canada peaked in membership and influence in the 1920s. In 1921, the population of Canada was just under 8,800,000. At that time, the Orange Order consisted of at least 100,000 members, with many more who had been through an Orange Lodge or were related to a member. As can be seen in Fig. 2.1, there were in excess of 2000 lodges in Canada at that time (Wilson 2007: 21). According to Wilson, four factors contributed to the functional decline of the Orange Order in Canada in the post-Second War period, notably in the 1960s. First, a burgeoning Canadian nationalism diminished the bonds of the British Empire. We can add here that in addition to this Canadian tendency, there were push factors from postcolonial and increasingly Euro-oriented political developments in Britain itself. Second, a rapidly developing ethnic diversity diluted the dualistic ethnic hold of Orangeism. Third, growing secularization—and we would add ethno-religious diversity—reduced the relevance of anti-Catholicism. Finally, the emergence of the welfare state, made necessary by the inadequacies of mutual and private provision in the Great Depression to provide employment and welfare assistance, undercut the fraternal and solidaristic roles of the Orange Order (Wilson 2007: 21). From having 82 lodges and 10,000 Orangemen in good standing in 1920, Toronto by 2005 had been reduced to a little over 250 Orangemen in nine lodges (Houston and Smyth 2007: 182).

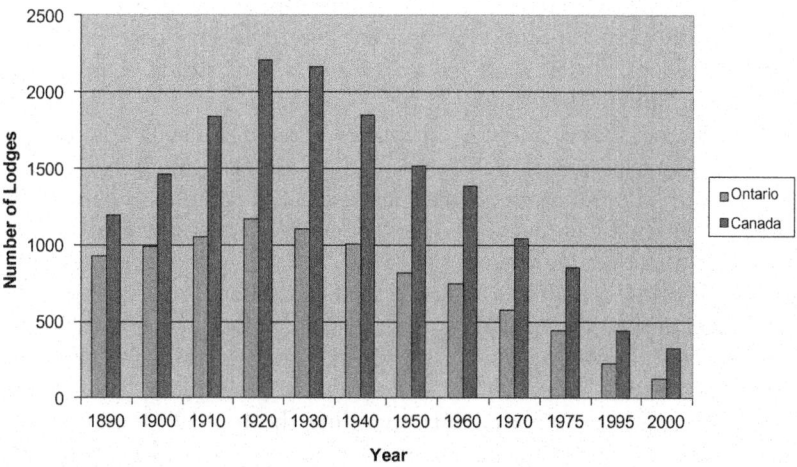

Fig. 2.1 Orange Lodges in Canada and Ontario 1890–2000

Typical of the growth and decline in membership is the report in *The Sentinel* of Spring 2009 (135-1), of the Diamond Lodge in Musgrave Harbour, Newfoundland. The lodge was founded with seven chartered members in 1877. At its peak, it had 379 members, finally closing in 1993 with six senior members. An anecdotal account of the decline in the Orange Order was the account of Orangeman, Joseph Clarke, who arrived in Canada from Ireland in 1924 (McConnell 2012). Both in County Monaghan and Toronto, Clarke was an active and leading member of a number of Orange Lodges. He deposited his Orange Lodge Certificate with Enniskillen L.O.L. 387 in Toronto. However, following the World War, as Orangeism declined in popularity, Clarke, like so many others, turned his focus to other fraternal organizations, joining both the Masonic Lodge and the Rotary Club. While the numerical decline of the Orange Order in the post-war period did not arrive immediately, and while Premier Lesley Frost, whose Progressive Conservative Party dominated Ontario politics throughout the 1950s, was a prominent Orangeman, the movement was in decline as its religious, national, ethnic, fraternal, and socioeconomic relevance faded. As late as the 1960s and 1970s, there still remained a sense of a robust—if limited—Orangeism in parts of Canada. In 1972, Senior referred to the continued force of Orangeism in New Brunswick and Newfoundland as well as Ontario strongholds around Brockville and Ottawa (Senior 1972: x–xi). By 1980, Houston and Smyth reported the remaining core of Orange Lodges in Ontario as being south of Ottawa in Leeds, Lanark, and Carleton counties (1980: 165).

The Orange Order was still sufficiently present in the 1970s to register as an object of attention in small local newspapers. An article and two letters in the *Clinton News-Record* serve as an illustration (Hanly 1975; Falconer 1975; Orange 1975). The article celebrates the formation of the Clinton Lodge on January 18, 1858. Describing the prominent men and the various sites of the lodge over the decades, the article portrays the lodge as well as the Ladies Orange Lodge as benevolent societies that reflect and promote good citizenship, family values, patriotism, and charitable works (Hanly 1975: 27). The letters are more contentious. Written in response to complaints regarding the July 12 Orange parade, they defend the Order against its critics. The year 1975 witnessed one of the last Orange parades in Clinton, and it is rumored that King Billy's horse was cheerfully loaned by a local Catholic farmer! Despite this, one letter details vandalism against the Orange hall on the July 12 weekend and defiantly asserts the Orange view of history: "…he [the writer of a letter complaining about the parade] didn't know what had happened before 1690 and things have been better since the Battle of the Boyne" (Falconer 1975: 4). The other letter speaks of: "…the defeat of King James and the atrocities toward mankind which took place during his rule of Great Britain" (Orange 1975: 4). Also addressed to the author of the letter complaining about the parade, it states: "…the so called 'zombies' you refer to, have no quarrel with any Catholic or any Roman Catholic church. Our fight was against King James and his terrible rule" (Orange 1975: 4). One of the letters also contains notes of some resignation and concern for the future:

> We all got to face the fact that in this present generation, it is harder to keep Christian organizations going … it is old-fashioned to open meetings with a scripture reading and prayer, when so many meetings open at the bar. The Orangeman will have to make some changes perhaps in the future but Orange Day will never die…. Boost us if you can, Knock us if you must, But don't forget us. (Falconer 1975: 4)

The Canada that surrounds the remaining Orangemen has become a liberal pluralist and proudly multicultural country. Its immigration system was radically deracialized in the passage of the 1976 Immigration Act. Within a decade, the ethno-racial profile of Canada's immigrants went from predominantly white European to predominantly BME (black and minority ethnic) non-European. The cultural and institutional context in which contemporary Orangeism operates is one of the widespread support for religious tolerance and recognition of minority community rights. As we shall see, Canadian Orangemen have learned to adapt their deeply held loyalist beliefs to contemporary values, practices, and institutional structures. Among the more striking symbolic manifestations of this trend is the sale of the former Dian Orange hall in Toronto to a Muslim organization. The building, whose windows are still in the shape of Orange arches, has been an Islamic centre for over 25 years (Smyth 2015: 271).

In the chapters to follow, we now turn our attention to the perspectives, values, and realities of Canadian Orangemen, in their own words. The next chapter, Chap. 3, begins with the confessional roots of Protestantism and Christianity among the participants.

References

Bumstead, J.M. "Thomas Scott." *The Canadian Encyclopedia*. http://www.thecanadianencyclopedia.ca/en/article/irish/. Last edited March 4, 2015. Accessed May 16, 2017.

Campbell, Kimberly. "Sports, Stories and Secularization: Canadian Protestantism at the Turn of the Twentieth Century." *The Graduate History Review*, (University of Victoria) 2 (2010): 19–30.

Clarke, B. "Religious Riot as Pastime: Orange Young Britons, Parades and Public Life in Victorian Toronto." In *The Orange Order in Canada*, edited by D.A. Wilson, 25-41. Four Courts Press: Dublin, 2007.

Durham, John George Lambton. *Lord Durham's Report: An Abridgement of Report on the Affairs of British North America*. Ottawa: Carleton University Press, 1982.

Falconer, F. "Orange". *Clinton News-Record*, Thursday July 31, 1975: 4.

Hanly, H.M. "Orange Lodge Founded by Wm. Murphy." *Clinton News-Record*, Thursday July 24, 1975: 27.

Houston, Cecil J. & William J. Smyth. *The Sash Canada Wore: A Historical Geography of the Orange Order in Canada*. Toronto: University of Toronto Press, 1980.

Houston, Cecil J. & Smyth, William J. "The Faded Sash: The Decline of the Orange Order in Canada, 1920–2005." In *The Orange Order in Canada*, edited by D.A. Wilson, 170–92. Four Courts Press: Dublin, 2007.

Jenkins, William. "View From 'the Hub of the Empire': Loyal Orange Lodges in Early Twentieth-Century Toronto." In *The Orange Order in Canada*, edited by D.A. Wilson, 128–45. Four Courts Press: Dublin, 2007.

Kaufmann, Eric. "The Orange Order in Ontario, Newfoundland, Scotland and Northern Ireland: A Macro-social Analysis." In *The Orange Order in Canada*, edited by D.A. Wilson, 42-68. Four Courts Press: Dublin, 2007.

Kealey, Gregory. "Orangemen and the Corporation: The Politics of Class in Toronto During the Union of the Canadas." In *Workers and Canadian History*, edited by Gregory Kealey, 163–208. Kingston: McGill-Queen's University Press, 1995.

MacRaild, Donald M. "The Associationalism of the Orange Diaspora." In *The Orange Order in Canada*, edited by D.A. Wilson, 25–41. Four Courts Press: Dublin, 2007.

McConnell, Brian. *An Ulsterman from County Monaghan*. Unpublished. Dated 19 May, 2012.

Orange. "Orangemen." *Clinton News-Record*, Thursday July 31, 1975: 4.

Pennefather, R.S. *The Orange and the Black: Documents in the History of the Orange Order Ontario and the West, 1890–1940*. Canada: Orange and Black Publications, 1984.

Radforth, Ian. *Royal Spectacle: The 1860 Visit of the Prince of Wales to Canada and the United States*. Toronto: University of Toronto Press, 2004.

Senior, Hereward. *Orangeism: The Canadian Phase*. Toronto: McGraw-Hill Ryerson, 1972.

Smyth, William J. *Toronto, the Belfast of Canada: The Orange Order and the Shaping of Municipal Culture*. Toronto: University of Toronto Press, 2015.

Thomson, A. (1983). *The Sentinel and Orange and Protestant Advocate, 1877–1896: An Orange view of Canada*. Theses and Dissertations (Comprehensive). Paper 10. Submitted in partial fulfilment of M.A. degree, Wilfrid Laurier University. http://scholars.wlu.ca/etd/10.

Toner, Peter and Gillian Leitch. "Irish Canadians." *The Canadian Encyclopedia*. http://www.thecanadianencyclopedia.ca/en/article/irish/. Last edited May 27, 2016. Accessed May 16, 2017

Wilson, D.A. "Introduction." In *The Orange Order in Canada*, edited by D.A. Wilson, Four Courts Press: Dublin, 2007, 9–24.

Wilson, D.A. "The Assassination of Thomas D'Arcy McGee." *The Canadian Encyclopedia*. http://www.thecanadianencyclopedia.ca/en/article/irish/. Last edited March 4, 2015. Accessed May 16, 2017.

CHAPTER 3

Faith

Abstract This chapter is an exploration of the core faith of contemporary Orangemen in Canada. This chapter begins with a brief account of the growth of Protestant religion in Canada, and then traces how members understand the role of religion in their lives. What role does this play in their social identities and their relations with others, most notably Roman Catholicism, but also the non-Christian religions of Islam, Hinduism, and Sikhism? It highlights members' own sense of social identity and the meaning given to religion in constructing Orangeism as a contemporary sense of belonging. It further explores the role religion plays in formulating a transnational identity comparing their views to similar groups in other societies, notably Northern Ireland.

Keywords Protestantism · Roman Catholicism · Islam · Religion and politics · Identity

The demographic basis of Orangeism in Canada is the migration of large numbers of Protestants from Ireland and Scotland throughout the early- to mid-nineteenth century. To begin, the main denomination among all Canadian Irish was Anglican, with Methodists following a prominent second and Presbyterians featuring as a majority only in some small parts of the country. The vast majority of emigrants came from Ulster, although north Leinster was also well represented (McAuley 1992). Throughout much of the early 1800s, absolute numbers of Irish migrants to British North America exceeded those to the USA, although the proportion of Catholic emigrants to Canada swelled during the 1830s and 1840s, driven by the famine.

When emigrants arrived, they encountered established settlement patterns with a strong Protestant base and ethos. Those who came to Ontario found themselves in a British and largely Protestant colony and helped guide and reformulate the initial ethnicity and identity of the diaspora. They encountered an embryonic Orange Order whose origins and initial development lay with the British military. One of the earliest records of such a military presence was found in Halifax in 1799, where soldiers, having been demobilized, settled in that part of the country and formed a Lodge. Together with immigrants from Ireland, they shaped and gave momentum to Orangeism and the underpinning of the Canadian Order. In a province that had already been given much of its focus and direction by the United Empire Loyalists' rejection of the new American republic, and which adopted a highly recognizable British and monarchist tone, the Orange Order flourished.

By the end of the nineteenth century, around half of entire Canadian membership was based in Ontario, and the Orange Order had become significant in Canadian society. About one-third of all English-speaking Canadians were members by the turn of the twentieth century, and Canada held more Orange Lodges under its jurisdiction than there were in Ireland. Orange Lodges quickly established a support system by which the transition of new migrants could be eased into their new society. They furnished much needed resources, delivering some level of welfare, functioned to take care of the sick and elderly, and later established an Orange widows pension and insurance scheme. For many, it was the Orange Lodge that provided the only counter to social suffering, which at least took the edge off some of the hardships of emigration.

At the core of Orange society was the church. Orangeism not only provided a focus and leadership to the rapidly growing numbers but it also offered a developing sense of religious cohesion within that community. Further, Orangeism provided a nucleus for the dominant colonial sentiments of Protestantism and loyalty to Britain to be publically expressed. This, of course, had broader consequences, manifesting in outpourings of anti-Catholicism and expressions of anti-republicanism.

It was against this background that many Irish Protestant emigrants refocused their sense of identity. Canada, of course, established its own

Orange folklore and traditions, but its symbolism was quickly recognizable to those most recently arrived from Ireland, and it was these factors which gave migration to Canada its particular Orange hue (Houston and Smyth 1980). The church continued to be an important feature in the formation of the cultural identity of Protestants, and the Orange Order was central in this process. The culture of Canadian Orangeism drew on a common set of values and styles of life that represented the familiar, but which became embedded in the distinct and separate culture. Nonetheless, it was a culture to which they could relate, even if it was several thousand miles from home. The values and culture of Orangeism that emerged were to prove extremely long-lasting in the history of English Canada. Underlying all of this was a belief in the Orange Order as a means of defending and promoting the Protestant faith. Many current members still regard it with a fierce loyalty and are particularly determined to promote its defense of Protestantism.

This chapter traces how members understand the role of religion in their lives and across the broader society, the function this plays in the construction of social identity, and what this means in terms of relations with others, most notably Roman Catholicism, but also non-Christian religions, such as Islam, Hinduism, and Sikhism. It highlights members' own sense of social identity and the meaning and significance given to religion in constructing Orangeism as a contemporary source of belonging. It further explores the role of religion for Canada Orangemen, and the part it plays in formulating a transnational identity, comparing their views to similar groups in other societies, most notably Northern Ireland.

So, what role does religion play for Orange members in contemporary Canada? The rules of the Order state that members should have: "a steadfast faith in Jesus Christ," and be: "a sincere observer of the Lord's Day, 'as well as being': a regular attendant at His House." In supporting the Protestant reformation, the Order's members (as elsewhere) are required to oppose the "false doctrines" of the Roman Catholic church. The Roman Catholic hierarchy is entirely rejected, alongside the universal claims of the Catholic church and doctrines such as papal infallibility, the immaculate conception, and the assumption of the Virgin Mary into Heaven. Orangemen regard such notions as having no basis in scripture, and subscription to the Order further requires the unambiguous denunciation of the idolatrous premises of the Roman Catholic church, according to Ian:

> ... when you say a mass, that's an abomination under the Lord because when his blood was shed he was finished on the cross, and when you—what you—so why would you sacrifice him over and over again, eh? That's totally wrong.

Canadian Orangemen, as Orangemen elsewhere, are required to: "strenuously oppose the fatal errors and doctrines of the Church of Rome" and "should, by all lawful means, resist the ascendancy of that church" (Orange Reformation PR Committee 2017). Whereas the Roman Catholic church places emphasis upon baptism as a means of salvation, Protestant belief stresses the roles of repentance and personal faith. The use of the Mass as the main mode of Roman Catholic worship, incorporating a belief in transubstantiation (that the body and blood of Christ are literally present), is seen as a total departure from the teachings of the Bible.

As Harold explained:

> ... in regards to the Protestant faith, we explain to them that we believe in the Trinity, the father, son, and holy ghost and that Jesus Christ is the only mediator between God and man, and the Saviour of mankind, and we tell them you know, that that's what we believe in and we would hope that that's what you believe in too.

Tom aired his views with regard to Catholicism as follows:

> ... the new Pope, he's making some of the right noises, but his message is right now getting very inconsistent, with what he's got in mind for his own church. My belief in Protestantism says that there is no man between me and my God ... which I see the Pope as [doing].

How widely are such doctrines interpreted by members of the Orange Order in Canada? To begin, we will consider broadly the issue of member's relationship with the church and the need for church attendance. The injunctions of the Order are, as we shall see, open to interpretation by many contemporary Orangemen, and while each of our participants is a Protestant, they vary considerably in their denomination and degree of devoutness and observance. Among those we interviewed were Anglicans and a member of the Salvation Army. Most, however, belonged to the United Church of Canada, a church that was created for pragmatic reasons in the 1920s, to service the growing number of remote communities across Canada. The United Church combined the Congregationalists, the Methodists, and the Presbyterians and has evolved into a liberal and progressive denomination, which may in part account for the variety of voices we heard among the membership.

Those we interviewed had mixed feelings regarding the desirability of habitual and consistent attendance at church. Some attended regularly and held doing so in high regard. Indeed, for Bill it remained an essential feature of being an Orangeman, part of the celebration of what he called his "Protestant heritage", arguing that: "The thing for me is that it's a celebration of your Protestant heritage. ... Like obviously we believe in the Protestant faith and I was raised in the church myself. I'm still—regularly attend church with my family."

Roy reflected such views and saw attendance at church in the following terms: "to a lot of Orangemen ... church is a very, very, strong part of it...." Indeed, there were those who were highly critical of fellow Orangemen for non-church membership or for not regularly attending their church. According to Mike:

> We would attend a church service if our Lodge did a service which we used to do periodically. All the members would come with their colours and it was a fantastic experience, but they didn't belong to a church of their own—the Lodge was the church—and every Wednesday you know you would come and you would have a sermon from the Chaplain—from the bible—and that was their religious experience.

Pete was, however, somewhat more restrained in his belief of what made a good Orangeman and whether church attendance formed a necessary part, saying:

> I wouldn't consider myself ... I don't know how to describe it ... devout ... I mean I go to ... I attend church ... I believe in God ... I believe in the Protestant faith. I believe in the Orange Order, but I wouldn't say I'm walking down the street knocking on doors and giving people the good news.

Mike, on the other hand, suggested that he was rather dismayed at the level of church attendance among members:

> ... one of the questions I used to ask when I went to meetings was how many people here in the room belong to a church? I actually got to the point where I stopped asking the question because it became a bit of an embarrassment for people.

Many participants, however, had a considerably more relaxed view of the need for regular church attendance in being an Orangeman, Clive claiming that: "I go (to church) the odd time," or this from Tom: "I'm not ... somebody who goes to church on any kind of regular basis." Other participants reported that they felt distanced, even disenfranchised, from their chosen church, expressing their disappointment at the direction taken by it in theological terms and in its everyday relationships with the Orange Order. Clive, who has strong Scottish Presbyterian roots, expressed his disenchantment that local churches refuse to allow Orange services in their churches:

> I'm disappointed in the Presbyterian churches here ... especially—because two different occasions they wouldn't let us hold a service in their church ... [St. Andrew's] let us in once—and the second time they said no. [The other] Presbyterian church said no. There's no point in even asking them.

Such views were broadly supported by a number of participants who made reference to the, at best, mixed reception that the Orange Order received in the Protestant churches. This perspective was reinforced by Dave, who gave another example of the Orange Order being deliberately misunderstood and ostracized in the area. He explained, the church:

> ... didn't want to upset the people in the area ... they thought it would be confrontational to the people in the area. That's what [named church] said ... we just wanted to go to church as a lodge ... you know sing the hymns [it's the] big Presbyterian church. They would get their information from the media—from the newspaper. Oh the Protestants they're anti-Catholic! Oh the bigots are coming!

There is some denominational variance, but, by and large, religiosity, as measured by frequent church attendance, is not noticeably high among the membership. Only a small minority of members regularly attend church.

This does not mean that participants underestimate religion as a factor in bringing members together or in providing a common sense of social identity and collectivity. Mike explains the sentiments of attachment to "Protestantism" that furnishes a sense of community and continuity, when he says:

> ... when I came to Canada I was aware of the fact that the Lodge was here, but I made no approach to it and joined the [United] church ... and children were baptized there and my oldest daughter walked her down the aisle there ... my faith was secured long before I left Scotland. I saw the church as a reinforcement—the United Church—but primarily it was a social gathering place.

He goes on to explain how at a particular Sunday service a fellow congregant invited him to join the Lodge. For this Orangeman as well as for other members, the Lodge played the role of a surrogate church and, to some extent, served as the place of ritual and meaning in his life:

> ... it was a social contact and it was a place that I could go to and be with the brethren—my brothers—the other members—and participate in a ritual which was very heavy on faith and consequently reminded me of that faith every time we had a meeting.

Mike continues:

> ... what I found, once I was in the Lodge, was that many of the members in those days ... came from the old country, from Ulster ... many of them while they were very strong in their faith of being Protestant [but] did not attend a church ... they didn't attend a church because they came from a country where the Lodge was the church ... and every Wednesday you know you would come and you would have a sermon from the Chaplain—from the bible—and that was their religious experience.

Other members simply felt that they didn't need to attend church to express their Protestantism and that the Lodge was an adequate substitute. Tom expands upon this theme: "I find the presence of the prayer in the Lodge meeting satisfying in a way that I can't really explain, but it's like, one of the reasons I am an Orangeman."

Some members openly expressed the notion of their commitment to Protestantism acting as guiding core belief and offering a broad system of moral guidance. It is drawn upon as to make sense of a world and an individual's place within it. Thus, Protestantism for Orange members provides an explanation and a set of values that help generate and explain a sense of order, and through a personal belief system position them in the world. Protestantism intentionally offers a set of beliefs, moral codes, and values which form the foundation of individual identity (Erikson 1963). This is evidenced in Tom's comment that:

> ... the role of Protestantism in Canada today ... well I think, in many ways it's like ... a system of morality ... centered on um, your belief in God ... and the after life ... I think that in a very secular society, that the Orange really is a beacon to those people that are looking for answers along that line, and certainly you ... can see where that is an attraction to our members.

or Dave's statement that: [Canada was] "founded on Christian principles—the Orange Order was a big part of that."

Keith expands upon the nature of Protestantism in this way:

> I believe the Protestant Faith has a strong, a strong influence on society when it's exercised but not always in the church because faith exercised in the church is your own personal expression of how you worship your God ... but at the same time through the Orange Association, the religion is expressed in many different ways in the Orange Association, there's our, our, our loyalties, which is expressed but it's based on a—we bring the religion into it and how we do that ... and, and in saying that, the Protestant faith has a strong influence in how I find my Protestantism and how I express it in public.

Understood in this way, Protestantism is used as a filter through which to judge contemporary affairs. Indeed, for Keith, his Orangeism and his understanding of Protestantism are synonymous, claiming that: "I think the Orange Association and my Protestant faith work hand in hand."

Two of the more obvious questions to ask are how the members see their commitment to being Protestant affecting their relationships with their Catholic neighbors, and whether the sectarian divisions, found most notably in Scotland and Northern Ireland are in any way reproduced in the contemporary Canadian context. There are, of course, many examples of historical sectarian conflict in Canada's past, and religious discord and disagreement were central to Canadian life until reasonably recently (Noll 1992). In the late nineteenth century, for example, denominational and religious differences were manifest in a wide range of public issues: Sunday observance, temperance, and the public funding and management of separate Catholic schools were all matters of some political controversy and public engagement. The legacy and continuing deliberation of such issues meant they had currency well into middle of the twentieth century, when Canadians were still among most church-going peoples in the world.

Do such divisions still have resonance with Orangemen in the contemporary period? Among participants, there is little or no hostility expressed toward Roman Catholics, and, in fact, many Orangemen go out of their way to express good relations or even friendship with Catholics in their immediate family or neighborhood. As Bill says: "because we're pro-Protestant doesn't mean we're anti-Catholic or the like."

Harold, an elderly and long-standing member, recalled the situation of his youth, and an event that has stayed with him:

> I went to high school and there was, there was no Catholic school in [named place] at that time, and we had, the Protestants and Catholics, we all went together. And I had a couple friends in high school and they were Roman Catholic, I mean they were. He didn't talk about my religion, I didn't talk about his, and we were the best friends. He would do anything for me, and I would do anything for him, but religion never came up. And you know I think it was, that more so, that way now where people didn't say, oh you're Catholic, you're Protestant, you—that, that doesn't matter. That's your personal business—on Sunday business—I don't think it should come up through the week or while you're at activities of any kind, I don't think that that should make one bit of difference … it don't matter whether you're, it's the same. It don't matter whether you're white, black, yellow, purple, what color your skin is, you're—we're all humans.

Another story of an Orange parade encountering a wedding at a Roman Catholic church was told to us on several occasions by different people to illustrate the nature of relations between the two denominations. It seems to have become deeply engrained in local Orange folklore. Phil recalls:

> And on the same day coming back along [named street] at the Catholic church there was a wedding going on … our guys were running over, getting their pictures taken with them … and they loved it, come over and take pictures … and the wedding came over and stood in the parade and took pictures with us, the wedding party, they were Roman Catholic church and they're coming … compare that to St. Patrick's church in Belfast.

According to Pete's version:

> … we walk right past St. Michael's Catholic cathedral and—do it every year and there was—what was it two years ago … we were walking past and there was a Catholic wedding going on—the wedding party came

out—and I think they were Italian—in fact I believe they were Italian—the church used to be very Irish Catholic—St. Michael's right?—which—St. Michael is a real patron saint of the Irish—there's not many Irish left there—mostly it's Italian and stuff like that—they came out and said "oh look at this." They jumped into the parade and had their picture taken ... Because everyone loves a parade—yeh everyone loves a parade.

Indeed, for many Orangemen unlike in Canada's past or in other places today, there seemed little restriction or sanction, formal or otherwise, on forming and maintaining relationships with Catholics. Members were aware of what this had meant in previous times. Phil told us the following story:

I had an uncle, well many of them, but a great uncle that was a member of the Orange Order in Toronto, he was a lecturer in his Lodge, his daughter married a [Catholic] French Canadian ... his name was Herb, and I said to my grandmother why, why did uncle Herb leave the Orange Lodge, he said because Viola married Harold.

Similarly, Keith had this tale of his family:

... one of my Grandfather's brother's sons married a Catholic, and they moved from Campbellford to Chicago ... to avoid the, to avoid the ridicule that they were facing ... because my grandfather, and his father, and two other senior members of that family travelled to Chicago, for what reason we do not know, but we suspect to lay a beating on the boy ... we're talking about the, the 1930's ... where they would actually travel to Chicago to prove a point, like you just ruined the family, no you didn't, you just made a life different from what the family chose. Now, the ridicule, but to run and then the chase, I can't, I can't stand it. And I would, If I knew that when Grandpa was alive, I would have had to have had a discussion with him on that right, but I didn't know that 'til after.

Today, such issues are in the most place far distant memories. Pete told us that "you can attend a Catholic wedding—you can attend a Catholic funeral and nobody gives you grief about it," and that "you can be married to a Roman Catholic" without any real comeback. Pete revealed:

... my best friend is a Jesuit priest—I have a Jesuit priest who's a friend of the family—we have him over for dinner every week—he knows what I am and I know what he is and we have the debate every single time—but it's always in good taste—always friendly and he always comes back for more so who knows, right?

Roy reports:

> I mean I have Roman Catholics in our family, you know we don't hate them. But Orangemen generally dislike the religion, at least that's what they are supposed to do, they're not supposed to dislike the people. If you dislike the people then you have a problem with, other, other than being Orange, because that's not the Orange approach, to dislike people themselves, it's to dislike something inherently wrong in their religion or something that they do.

Mike takes a pragmatic approach to such issues:

> ... you know—we can't penalize a person for marrying a Roman Catholic because if that person marries a Roman Catholic in a civil process she is no longer a Roman Catholic—if the member married her in a Catholic ceremony, he's no longer going to be a member.

Such changing attitudes were often explained in generational terms, with the younger members often portraying themselves as having a more liberal interpretation to such matters. Representing the younger generation, Pete says:

> I know guys who are married to Roman Catholics—it's not—it's not—you know you're not given a high five by the older crew I'm sure—but that's mostly the older crew and I mean—they're 80 and how much more time do they have left? It's a dying generation—so it's not really an issue for us—I do go and I have gone to Catholic funerals—my grandmother was Catholic—she passed away—I met three or four bishops there—Catholic bishops and they all know who I am ... I put orange flowers at the funeral—but they know—I put orange lilies at all of the funerals.

In telling of the Catholic wedding and the interaction with an Orange Parade outlined above, Pete completed his story with the following comment: "...the Grand Master was looking at us—he's from Scotland—he said 'this would never happen in Coatbridge ... it would never happen in Coatbridge'."

Roy expressed it rather more directly, referring to those with fixed attitudes and "traditional" attitudes in the organization, he said: "So they're living in the 1920's and 1930's a lot of them ... and they haven't got to anywhere else."

This notion of generational change was raised during several of the interviews. Here, Keith puts forward such views when he says:

> ... like I'm new generation—my father wasn't involved—so a lot of those old prejudices weren't there—and that reminds me somebody would say "well we're not getting members because people think we're bigots"— Wrong! The bad news is nobody knows who we are—the good news is, nobody knows who we are—we have a clean slate to reinvent ourselves— so personally when [Mike] and I talk—the core principles—freedom of religion and political choice, those are what we build on ... those are the core principles ... how you relate those is actually another matter.

Several compared this situation directly with that found in Northern Ireland, and Charles was keen to point to differences between Northern Ireland and Canada on the Catholic issue: "Well, I don't agree with condemning the Catholics like they do ... I have my daughter-in-law who is a Catholic and my—one of my nieces is [Catholic]." Don made this broad point:

> Now the Grand Lodge of Ireland still has that on their books. And the Charter of Rights and Freedoms in Canada forbids you from penalizing a person for your spouse's—you know—religion—and indeed we can no longer ask that question in the application—and they [Orangemen from Northern Ireland] don't always take a good view of that—um but it's sort of—it's just a difference...between our reality and their reality.

While Keith simply could not comprehend the relationships that existed elsewhere:

> ... the difference being as I would understand it, Ian Wilson, past Grand Master of Scotland only just got the Constitution changed in Scotland to allow a member to attend a funeral in a Catholic church for a friend. I don't believe that, I've been to funerals of a lot of people and I don't believe any member of the Orange Association who had a friend who was a Roman Catholic or of any other faith, that would not attend that person's funeral, based on the fact I'm an Orangeman [that] I can't do that because I'm an Orangeman. ... I don't believe that exists.

While Don had the following to say in comparing the situation in Canada to Northern Ireland:

> Now I haven't had the experience of being there [Northern Ireland] but from what I see they get into these conflicts on a—on a fairly regular basis. I've never known of that happening in Canada. We're a little bit—what do you say—we're a little bit—maybe we seem more liberal on that point like … we don't condemn the Roman Catholics in Canada.

The issue of context is vital here. Pete told us part of his life history, which in the context of other areas of Orange strength, such as Scotland or Northern Ireland, is extraordinary:

> … actually a twist to this story is that my mother's Roman Catholic, my Uncle's a priest—my Aunt a nun—so it wasn't very easy for me to become an Orangeman—er it wasn't easy to tell them I was going to be an Orangeman– so when I was growing up I went to Catholic school … I went to Catholic church … I went to church on Sunday—I didn't know any better—but I also went to Anglican church and Anglican Sunday school—I went to both because you know I went with my grandmother once in a while, I went with my parents once in a while … So, what it ended up being is choice … choice on my part.

While there remains some anti-Catholic sentiment, and in the case of a few members fairly vitriolic views, this is usually expressed in terms of being against the Catholic church and its doctrine, rather than against individuals. One member, who proudly expressed his monarchist views (and was a member of the Monarchist League), claimed not to be anti-Catholic and spoke generally of the good relations between Catholics and Protestants in Canada. He noted wryly that the existing Orange hall is rented from the Catholic separate school board and is adjacent to a Catholic elementary school. He did, however, go on to lament the tendency among new arrivals from Northern Ireland to drop their religion and their loyalism.

In so doing, he presented Catholicism as something of a Trojan horse, seemingly benign, but in fact a threat to Protestantism. He regarded the Protestant faith as in need of protection. Others expressed varying levels of disdain for Roman Catholicism, Phil proudly declaring that: "I am 65, I've been in the Catholic church a grand total of once in my life and it was for a Wedding and I thought I had to be there." Pete said he had fundamental problems with the Catholic church, but continued: "I have no animosity or hatred towards Catholics—that's what most people think the Orange Lodge has—is some kind of animosity or hate—they can't call me hateful."

Bill recalled his visit to Northern Ireland and was genuinely amazed by what had happened:

> A true thing happened to me when I was in, in Northern Ireland. I stopped at a bed and breakfast, it was full, so ... I asked the gentlemen, where's another bed and breakfast? Go down to the intersection about a mile down and turn right, third house on the left. OK, so I backed out of the laneway and just as I pull ahead, right next door is a bed and breakfast ... pulled in there, went in, sure enough they had rooms, the lady had a room ... but as soon as you walk in there's a crucifix there, there's a crucifix there. He wouldn't send me to her, because she was a Roman Catholic, and he was a Protestant.

It is a tale that anyone who lives in Northern Ireland will regard as commonplace, part of the localized sectarian mosaic that makes up social and political relations in that part of the world. Indeed, we would suggest it would barely draw comment from anyone from there and is just another part of the everyday. But for Bill, viewing it through the eyes of a Canadian Orangeman, such goings on were extraordinary and clearly worthy of comment.

Dave was keen to debunk what he saw as some of the fallacies of what happened at his local lodge meetings:

> ... some people have said to me: "all you do in Orange Order meetings is talk about Catholics," and that's the furthest thing from the truth—I'm sure you've all heard it—all they see is talking about the Fenians as they say. We don't, it's not true ... there's not much talk of Catholics—No! My goodness it's amazing—my wife thought that I did this.

Clive, another long-standing member, had this to say:

> [The Orange Order has] been referred to in some papers as the—the Irish KKK—I seen that ...Yes the Orange Order and that brings a bit of a racial thing into it.... I guess you probably know in Togo there's a lodge which is made up of black members. And then a little bit up north here in Deseronto too—there's a Mohawk [Indigenous American] Lodge which is.... So to say we're anything like the KKK is—it's just ridiculous.

All of those interviewed for this book were white men, but all were adamant that there was nothing to disbar people of color from joining the Order. Dave put it as follows:

> ... if somebody ... a good Protestant (of colour) ... came along and said I'd love to join you, and I'll abide by all the rules and everything, I'd be comfortable with that.... We'd say "this guy, he goes to his church, he works in the community and whatever—he believes in the Orange Order." Do you think we're going to say no?

Overall, the situation is largely one of moderation and tolerance toward Catholics. Certainly, the highly politicized forms of sectarianism found in Northern Ireland and, to a lesser extent, Scotland are absent in Canada. Broadly, there is a generalized acceptance and even respect accorded to Catholics among the Orangemen. A number of participants draw contrastive parallels between the treatment accorded to Catholics and Catholicism in Ulster as well as in the history of the Canadian Orange Order and conclude that the contemporary Orange Order in Canada is far more enlightened. Orangemen are married to Catholics, have Catholic children and in-laws, Catholic friends, or casual acquaintances, and share some informal fraternal camaraderie with Catholic brotherhoods, notably members of the Knights of Columbus. The Knights of Columbus, a Catholic fraternal organization that many regard as the Catholic equivalent of the Orange Order, is frequently invoked as an admirable and parallel organization. Keith goes so far as to say:

> So personally, I'm always a little more comfortable dealing with a person of faith—I really don't care what their faith is. I Couldn't care less what their faith is ... because at least we ... we're on common grounds that we believe in something greater than ourselves ... so it keeps things in perspective and a little bit of humility—whatever that was.

There is then a far greater diversity of views toward Roman Catholics that one might expect from Orange Order members; certainly, it is in contrast to the views held by Orangemen elsewhere. The most common reference and point of comparison among respondents was that of Northern Ireland. But the social and political contexts are very different, not least because of relations in Northern Ireland being influenced by local competition with Catholics in ways they are not in Canada. As Pete put it: "here we don't have the same rules ... as in Northern Ireland."

The degree to which Canada is different and the same rules don't apply is worthy of some consideration. Religion still plays an important role among Canadian Orangemen. Members do make the consistent claim that they are opposed to the doctrines of the Roman Catholic church but are equally keen to suggest that do not feel any hostility to individual Roman Catholics, despite the Orange Order's uncompromising rejection of the doctrines and practices of that church. Underpinning much of this is the interpretation of the biblical message that salvation is to be found through the relationship an individual has with Christ. Some Canadian Orangemen still no doubt see these issues as central to their being. Set in the context of a contemporary secular Canadian society, however, where the lack of overt sectarianism or the tying of Protestantism directly to a sense of national identity is noteworthy, it means a different, gentler form of social relationships can be constructed between Catholics and Protestants than, for example, found in Scotland or Northern Ireland.

What then of relations with other religions and the place of religion in Canada? Recent times have seen a steady rise in Canada's non-Christian religious population, from 4% in 1991 to 8% in 2011. Today, these smaller religious groups account for more than one in ten Canadians, up from just under one in twenty around 30 years ago. Moreover, Christian groups have witnessed a sizable decline in their shares, from 47% to 39% over the past 40 years. Within this, those identifying as Protestants have diminished fairly dramatically from 41% to 27% (Pew Research Center's Forum on Religion and Public Life 2013). There has also been a sizable decline in religious commitment in the Canadian population. As recently as 1986, more than 40% of Canadians claimed they were regular attendees at religious services (at least once a month), but by 2010, this figure had fallen to 27% (Pew Research Center's Forum on Religion and Public Life 2013).

The rise of those identifying as having no religion is also noteworthy, and here, there are clear differences across the generations. In 2011, some 29% of Canadians born between 1967 and 1986 expressed no religious affiliation whatsoever, which is 17 points higher than those born in 1946, or earlier. In addition, this gulf between younger and older Canadians appears to be increasing. In 1971, the percentage of Canadians with no religious affiliation was fairly fixed across society, that is, it was roughly similar among younger, middle-aged, and senior adults. But today, 29% of young adults (ages 25–44) expressed no religious affiliation, contrasted with 20% some of those in middle age (ages 45–64) and only 12% of those aged 65 and over (Pew Research Center's Forum on Religion and Public Life, 2013).

This trend is, of course, not peculiar to Protestants, as Keith notes:

> I've got a really good friend in Knights of Columbus and he's very religious and he's quite upset that most Knights of Columbus don't go to church—a lot of people don't understand like with Catholics in particular and what with the Jewish faith—most people are Jewish by tradition, by culture not by religion and so [he] is really upset that most of the Knights don't go to church.

Nonetheless, the move away from the Christian churches and the move toward secularism are of concern. These are all worrying drifts for Orangemen, and particularly those who take seriously claims that Orangeism is about defending their religious beliefs its position in society. The move away from Canada as essentially a Christian country is taken seriously as is the move to secularism and growing number of those expressing no religion as a preference.

Nevertheless, those of a different religion are normally treated with great respect. Take this from Dave, a former factory worker and union member, who is making specific reference to fellow trade union members making disparaging remarks about Sikhs:

> I mean whenever I was going through the education with the Union up at Port Elgin, and people were saying: "now these Sikhs, they stick the knife in you." They got a speaker there and he was Sikh and their values are the same as ours. But what you get is "Turban head" and I hate that, you know? How many do you know? They're all God's children. I found them to be very similar to be honest. That was my experience.... I think the basics of something like the Orange Order—and probably the basics of some of their organizations—would probably be very similar).

Keith expressed his ecumenical view of the world as follows:

> In society ... when you embrace other people in your life you don't circle yourself with only Orange men in your neighbourhood, you live in a very ... wide variety of Ukrainians across the street, we have, I have an Italian next door that is a war vet, that doesn't like the British because he was a prisoner of war, and stuff like this so, and so and things, but when you talk

to them, you talk to them based on a very general understanding that you have your faith, I have my faith, you see things this way and this is how I see things, and everybody is happy to do that ... in some cases, some faiths don't allow you to be that ... some faiths I believe are very, very.... I'm trying to avoid to use the word narrow, but it is very narrow minded and what you can accept within society, and stuff like this ... no body is right, my faith is right for me. And if I find a hundred people like me, then that's a church. The idea is to listen to everybody's understanding of what their faith is, and what society is, and to offer the, when you have the opportunity, to impose or to express yours, to do it in a way that's not offensive, not derogatory, or not insulting, and to do that....

One exception to this broad point was found in the attitude to Islam, where rather more mixed attitudes were expressed by a section of the members, with a number of Orangemen displaying commonly held anti-Muslim sentiments. One Orangeman made reference to Muslims, portraying them as a community that forcibly insists on having its culture respected and its share of entitlements. This extends even as far as "reverse discrimination." Other Orangemen argued that Muslims and people from "other countries" bring their issues to Canada and do not value the Crown and all that Orangemen see it standing for.

Some Orangemen are particularly aggrieved by Muslims, who they regard as receiving special consideration and treatment, a theme that echoes past conflicts with Catholics claiming equal rights, which Orangemen viewed as special privileges. There is a perception among a few of the Orangemen that certain immigrants, notably Muslims, wish to attack Western and Christian culture in general, including the Protestant tradition. With regard to Muslim immigrants, Bill says: "... there's one particular religion that comes into Canada and it's opposed to every other religion—you know but because we're seen as—you know Western culture is a Christian culture, you know it's just—their whole thing is not to come here and integrate—it's to come here and defeat." There is a pervasive sense among some of the Orangemen both that new immigrants do not appreciate and support Canadian heritage and traditional values and that those who do, Orangemen included, are marginalized and silenced.

When asked: "is it the Muslims you're thinking of," Bill responds: "Yeah ... that's my opinion, I don't know—I think it would be—All Christian organizations Christians in general—but not specifically Protestants—so—so they'd be—they'd also dislike the Catholics just as much."

Harold went so far as to say: "I think that the real threat in Canada today is from some of these Muslim groups even more so than Rome, you know?"

These points were strongly made but were far from uniformly accepted in the group we interviewed. Keith, for example, said this:

> ... you can discuss with people of the Muslim faith, of the Catholic faith, of any other, or even those that have no faith at all, how you express yourself and I think that my faith is instrumental in that ... the answer is I believe in God and Jesus Christ and the Trinity and all of this and stuff like this and that's my personal point of view.

Or this from Bill:

> ... although we strongly believe in what our heritage and our culture and our faith is, we also respect other people although they're different—like you know—that's—that's their belief and you know like for myself—somebody believes in the Protestant faith.

Nonetheless, the result of such concerns regarding Islam has for some Orangemen been a dramatic change in discourse. While, of course, each Orangeman is a Protestant, and their faith finds a wide range of expression, many Orangemen have now spontaneously begun to refer to themselves as Christians rather than Protestants, and their points of reference are frequently associated with a more general Christianity. Roy explained this as follows:

> ... the word Christian seems to be coming into play more, and more, and more as opposed to Protestant. Now at one time when I was a boy ... it was common knowledge, and to be understood that Catholics were not Christians, and when you talk to them they did not want to be called Christians, they never wanted to be called Christians. This is a phenomenon of the last ten fifteen years, now Catholics want to be called Christians, they are part of the Christian community ... Now there's this peace, love and understanding thing that goes on.

Others refer to the inhibitions surrounding wishing people a "Merry Christmas" and the stripping away of Protestant symbolism in public spaces, attacking heritage and traditions. As Don explains:

> From what our culture is now to what it was even 10 years ago, I think it's changed. I see Canada as a kind of Christian-Judeo country and we've never had issues with Jews celebrating Hanukah—they've never had issues with us celebrating Christmas. Now if people work for a retailer and they wish a customer a Happy Christmas, they can be fired ....

Bill made much of the recent decisions to ban the Lord's Prayer from political assemblies and made the more general point that in his judgment, the Orange Order is seriously misunderstood, stereotyped as prejudiced and bigoted, and said that being a Christian in public is "almost mocked" and "it's almost seen as a sign of weakness." Being a Protestant is, in Bill's words, "seen as being intolerant." He says: "...to me—the Protestant religion is important in my life and its here maintaining that and to me there's a bit of an attack against the Protestant faith in Canada—like Christian faith in general."

For Don, what was going on represented a chipping away at the values and undermining of Protestantism and tradition in Canada:

> It's not everything at one time, like we're going to do away with the Protestant faith all in one go. It's brick by brick. You know we've lost scripture reading in school, we've lost the singing of our national anthem in a lot of schools, you know, they don't pledge allegiance or anything like that anymore. It's just slowly, like all our values are slowly—our history as far as the military goes is almost unknown. Like I've heard people on the radio say Canada has no military history. It's like are you kidding me?

In response, he and others urge a more robust defense of Protestantism and associated values in the public sphere led by the Orange Order. Religion remains of crucial importance to many Canadian Orangemen, and Protestantism continues to be an important feature in the formation of the cultural identity of Orange Order members. Religion can be thought of as forming a central element of their social identity and positioning their sense of self into inclusive social units. Many current members constantly refer back to a golden age, whether they are old enough to have experienced it or not, and the potential for releasing traditional Orange principles and to a degree religious fervor, which they believe lies buried in the consciousness of many Canadians. But these are difficult times for Canadian Orangemen. Christianity and religiosity are both in decline in Canada, and Orangemen are struggling to come to terms with changes to something that was once integral to the everyday. The Protestant religion is still the crucial delineator in defining group commonality and identity, but other cultural markers are also important. These draw on a range of rituals, practices, and institutions which seek to emphasize not just religion but also emphasize a shared British past and reflect the distinctiveness of Canada's history. The Protestant faith of Orange adherents provides a boundary marker between them and the other. Largely, this means Catholics, although this manifests as a very banal and non-assertive type of sectarianism, certainly compared to Northern Ireland. The "other" includes additional religious groups, especially Muslims who are seen as removed from Canadian culture. The current growing social acceptance of forms of Islamophobia and anti-Muslim sentiments blends a religious contrast readily into the more traditional enmities of Orangemen toward those who represent perceived threats against the British way of life, the Crown, and the forces of law and order. In the next chapter, we explore Canadian Orangemen's perspectives on the monarchy and the Crown, which, along with the Protestant faith, are core facets of Orange loyalism.

References

Erikson, Erik H. *Childhood and Society*. 2nd edition. New York: Norton, 1963.
Houston, Cecil J. & William J. Smyth. *The Sash Canada Wore: A Historical Geography of the Orange Order in Canada*. Toronto: University of Toronto Press, 1980.
McAuley, James W. "Under an Orange Banner: Reflections on the Northern Protestant Experiences of Immigration." In *The Irish Worldwide: History, Heritage, and Identity*, edited by Patrick O'Sullivan, 43–69. Leicester: Leicester University Press, 1992.
Noll, Mark A.L. *A History of Christianity in the United States and Canada*. Grand Rapids. Mich.: W.B. Eerdmans, 1992.
Orange Reformation PR Committee (2017). Pamphlet. Unpublished.
Pew Research Centre for Religion and Public Life (2013). 'Canada's Changing Religious Landscape' Report, 27 June 2013.

CHAPTER 4

Crown

Abstract This chapter presents views and perspectives on the monarchy. This includes values and beliefs surrounding the monarchy, both as a cultural symbol and as a constitutional principle. This chapter begins with an explanation of the meaning of the Crown for Canadian Orangemen and continues with an assessment of the impact of the recent pro-monarchist Conservative government on the Canadian Orange Order. This chapter explores the monarchy and multiculturalism, ethno-racial diversity, and adherence to certain symbolic rituals, such as singing the Royal Anthem and pledging allegiance to the Queen. This chapter concludes with an exploration of the personalization and modernization of the monarchy and its impact on Canadian Orangemen.

Keywords Crown · Monarchy · Canadian Constitution · Conservative Party of Canada · Multiculturalism

At the very core of Orangeism is a fidelity and loyalty to the Protestant Crown. The founding event and focus of collective memory and commemoration for Orangeism is the victory of King William of Orange, the Protestant monarch, in the Battle of the Boyne in 1690. Without the tribal loyalties and fealties of this personal pledge of allegiance and the associated commemorations of chosen glories and chosen traumas (Volkan 2001), there is no coherence at the heart of Orangeism. It is therefore not surprising that each of the Canadian Orangemen we interviewed, as well as the pages of *The Sentinel*, manifest deep and widespread loyalty to the monarchy.

Despite this sense of attachment to the Crown, loyalism in the contemporary Canadian context has undergone a range of important adaptations that speak to the constitutional and political cultural facets of contemporary Canada. The official Orange position on the monarchy is articulated in this recent publication from the Grand Orange Lodge:

> The Monarchy in Canada continues to uphold our traditions and heritage and recognizes all the Canadian excellence and achievements throughout the British Commonwealth and other nations. This Royal Family is a symbol of national unity representing all that is most admired not only representing our past but our future. We as Canadian Orangemen hold an esteem [sic] place of honour in our hearts as Queen Elizabeth continues to be the Defender of the Protestant Faith. It is the Crown that maintains peace and freedom that we so enjoy. (Grand Orange Lodge 2011: 10)

Support for the monarchy is an integral facet of a more generalized political conservatism and traditionalism, which also manifests itself in an even more pronounced support for the military and Canada's war heritage. Canadian Orangemen frequently reference the heritage of war heroes in Orange history and the central identity claim of being descended from those who "fought for our freedoms." This is in part replicated across the Orange world, witness the information leaflet published by the Grand Orange Lodge of Ireland in recent times entitled, "Battles Beyond the Boyne" (no date). It gives eight major facts about "Orangemen in Service," among which are that: "Up to a quarter of a million Orangemen served in the First World War, 80,000 of them from Canada alone" and that "There were so many Orangemen in one Canadian battalion, from Manitoba, that the battalion was nicknamed 'The Orange Battalion'."

Related to this is the colonial theme of British Canadianism (Champion 2010; Buckner 2005; Smith 1994; Hillmer and Chapnick 2007), a connection which is deemed to be under siege, and the determination of the contemporary Orange Order to attach itself to this glorified past, even in the face of opposition. Associated with support for the monarchy, the armed forces, and the British connection is a set of other traditional and conservative values, including those associated with law and order, economic conservatism, and traditional patriarchal values. As we have seen in Chap. 3, the connection to the Protestant faith itself is more nuanced and complex.

There has been a recent revival of the British Canadian heritage in Canadian historical analysis, popular culture, and among the Conservative Party political elite (Nesbitt-Larking and McAuley, forthcoming). A number of historians have made the point that what is claimed by liberals as a radical break within Canada from colony to nation and as the birth of an independent Canada conceals a continuation of deeply rooted British connections. In so doing, these authors have contributed to the reassertion of a confident and proud Britishness that in the view of some had been in decline (Buckner 2005; Champion 2010). They call for Canadian history to reclaim the central role of empire in the history of Canada, even if not always to celebrate it. Those who have popularized their views go further into the normative claims that rather than be ashamed of the monarchy, God Save the Queen, the Union Jack, the armed forces, and other elements of British Canadianism, Canadians, they argue, should be positively celebrating such symbols.

The former Prime Minister of Canada Stephen Harper, and his Conservative government, was a keen champion of a return to British values. According to John Ibbotson, the former Conservative government was:

> ...bent on transforming the idea of Canada, by changing the national myth. Many of this country's most cherished symbols and values—the flag, the Charter of Rights and Freedoms, peacekeeping, public health care, multiculturalism—are the product of Liberal policies. The Harper government seeks to supplement, or even supplant, those symbols with new ones, and old ones revived. These new symbols are rooted in a robust, even aggressive nationalism that celebrates the armed forces, the monarchy, sports, the North and a once overshadowed Conservative prime minister [Diefenbaker]. (Ibbitson 2012)

Among other moves, the Harper government placed great emphasis on restoring the central role of the monarchy, devoted major resources to royal tours, renamed the Canadian Museum of Civilization as the Canadian Museum of History, reworked the Citizenship Act and regulations to ensure greater anglo-conformity, and recreated the military as three distinct armed forces, now renamed as the "Royal" navy and air force (Nesbitt-Larking and McAuley, forthcoming). The emphasis on Canadian peacekeeping was replaced with a celebration of a more robust militarism and the chosen traumas and chosen glories of past military sacrifices and triumphs (Volkan 2001). While Canada under the Conservatives remained a multicultural polity that encouraged immigration, it became more selective and more assertive in the promotion of a cultural conformity that privileged possessive individualism, law and order, a Judeo-Christian moralism, and the British connection. As Charlotte Gray wrote, the Harper: "government is engineering a comeback for the monarchy" and the Prime Minister had a: "campaign to restore the symbols of an older, whiter Canada" (2012). Gray made reference to:

> a larger campaign, led by a group of fierce monarchists, including Harper's principal secretary, Ray Novak; John Baird; and Chris Champion, senior advisor to immigration minister Jason Kenney. These men make no secret of their eagerness to erase the Liberal-dominated narrative of recent Canadian history, with its emphasis on the Charter, multiculturalism, and the flag, and replace it with other, older traditions that embrace military victories and historical identification with Britain. (Gray 2012)

How far did such important developments resonate with Canadian Orangemen? Did these distinctive and definitive policy shifts embolden or enliven the Orange Order in Canada? The counterintuitive answer to these questions is that they appear not to have made much difference. Among the respondents, references to Harper are mixed, and there is at best a level of grudging and default support, along the lines of the Conservative Party being a more attractive proposition than the alternatives. Some participants speak disparagingly of Stephen Harper and do not regard him or his government as allies of the Orange Order. Roy regards Harper as having sold out English Canada to Quebec and its interests. As he says: "Quebec runs Canadian politics." In Mike's view: "I don't think their heart is in it," and others express a generalized distrust of all politicians and a reluctance to differentiate one from the other.

This curious absence of engagement and collaboration from two organizations that might be considered to have aligning interests is explained in part by the nature of the Orange Order itself. It is also a reflection of the current dwindling political relevance of the Orange

Order. In contrast with the nineteenth and early twentieth centuries, when the Orange Order had a large membership, was politically connected, and represented mainstream views, the current Orange Order is very small, with a declining membership of largely working-class and lower middle-class men, and to the extent that it has any visibility, is deemed to hold controversial and marginal views. The Conservative government neither needed nor wanted the support of the Orange Order, and it is probable that the movement was not even on its radar. From the perspective of the Orange Order, the pro-monarchist policy shifts of the Harper Conservatives were not visible and were crowded out by attention to other aspects of government policy that Orangemen disliked. From our interviews, it is apparent that there was very little contact between the Orange Order and the Harper government, and no special access was granted to Orangemen in Ottawa.

Despite this absence of mutual support and common purpose, the general perspective of Canadian Orangemen has remained conservative and traditional in nature. Orangemen are generally well-informed of the constitutional history of Canada and, in particular, the foundational efforts of the United Empire Loyalists to sustain British North America, a project that continued in modified form through the creation of Canada under the British North America Act (now the Constitution Act) of 1867. Canadian Orangemen are proud of the key roles played by Orangemen in the securing of Canada's loyalty to the British Empire and the creation of Dominion status. Arguably, the most prominent Orangeman is Sir John A. Macdonald, the architect of Canadian confederation and the first Prime Minister of Canada. Keith links the monarchy to Canada's distinctiveness as a constitutional order: "…Canadians really want to distinguish—have a separation from Americans—and that's one of the things unique about a Canadian—is that we do have the Queen as head of state." With regard to the monarchy, Clive says: "It's what Canada is—it's part of our heritage—sure—that's what made our country the country that it is." We invited the participants to reflect on the singing of God Save the Queen, the Royal Anthem, and the extent to which such a symbolic act should be required for Canadians (see full list of interview prompts in Appendix C). Of Canadians in the past, Bill recalls that "they did it in school … they were proud singing God Save the Queen."

With reference to the broader traditions of Orangeism, connections between faith and the Crown are frequently identified. With regard to the obligations of those who join the Orange Order, Harold says:

> ...and then of course the other thing in regards to the Protestant faith, we explain to them that we believe in the Trinity, the father, son, and holy ghost, and that Jesus Christ is the only mediator between God and man, and the saviour of mankind, and ... you will have to take an obligation to Queen, country, and the Protestant faith. You know and it's the morals of the faith that, you know, we think is the fabric of the country....

Roy expresses concern that: "unbeknownst to most people in Canada, nobody in Canada even understands that they have passed this article saying that the Queen or the King does not have to be a Protestant anymore. That has never made the news...." It is possible that Roy is referring to the British and Commonwealth Succession to the Crown Act of 2013, based on the Perth Agreement, that removed the disqualification of those who married Roman Catholics from the line of succession. Irrespective of the veracity of his claims, Roy is concerned that: "...the King or Queen can be a Catholic once again, and they're going to ... greatly impact the Orange Order."

European Canada has been a bilingual and, until recently, largely bicultural state, in which the ethno-linguistic traditions of the French and the English have been in balance. The orientation of the Orange Order toward Quebec and the French presence in Canada have been mostly oppositional and hostile. Associated with the Catholic church and disloyalty toward the British connection and the Crown, Quebec has come to be viewed with disfavor and suspicion. Gavin identifies Quebec as a part of the country that is "not monarchist in any sense of the word." With reference to anti-monarchical sentiments across Canada, Dave does not believe that there is a large movement to get rid of the monarchy, except "maybe in Quebec." Harold reminds us of the critical importance of the Crown in those anglophone enclaves of Quebec that were hegemonic in asserting anglo-conformity throughout the nineteenth and early twentieth centuries, in this personal narrative of his childhood in the one-room schoolhouse:

> ...when I went to school, grade one and two, it was a one-room school ... [they] taught grade one to eight, and I used to walk through the bush

a mile up to the school, and anyways, first thing we would—and this is in the Province of Quebec—the first thing we did would be the Lord's Prayer and then we'd sing Onward Christian Soldiers, then we sang The Queen, and then there was always—at that time when I went, it was the King ... his picture was up there and the big Union Jack—and when I was in grade one and two, I guess the teacher didn't know what to do with us, because she had to teach the other grades, and she'd say to us, okay now, you draw that Union Jack and colour it, and I don't know how many times I drew that Union Jack and coloured it, but you know that's—I was going to school in the Province of Quebec.

If Quebec and French Canada have been associated with indifference or hostility toward the Crown in a largely bicultural Canada, the orientation of more recent Canadians, part of the multicultural fabric of Canada, has been more mixed. From the perspective of certain Orangemen, the monarchy in the Commonwealth has long been associated with support for multiculturalism and ethno-racial diversity. Such a perspective is compatible with traditional conservative values that were grounded in elite accommodation of community leaders, adherence to broadly communitarian values, and a paternalistic *noblesse oblige*. Under such a regime, the earliest enthusiasts in support of multiculturalism in Canada were Prairie Conservatives, who regarded the policy as a needed corrective to what they viewed as unwarranted (over) accommodation of French Canada. Under multiculturalism, all ethnicities across Canada would be recognized, and not just the French and English "Charter Groups." Against such an openness toward multiculturalism is the more dominant conventional perspective that new immigrants are largely ignorant of and unsympathetic toward the Crown, and that they may represent a threat to the core values of tradition and loyalism that are defended by Orangeism. The same ambivalence may be seen in Orangemen's attitudes toward indigenous peoples and the Crown.

Dave is a leading member of an Orange hall in one of Toronto's multicultural suburbs in which the majority of residents are non-white, and immigration from Asia is high. As if addressing his minority neighbors, Dave says:

> ... this is not our [Orangemen's] Queen, but she is your [Commonwealth citizens'] Queen. You know she's not my Queen, yet you have a Queen here and she costs you nothing, 'cos you don't contribute to the Royal Family. We have a Queen [in Canada] but we don't contribute to nothing,

and then she comes here and you pay for the visit and stuff. Being multicultural ... especially this city ... the interest isn't there. The interest peaked during all the celebrations of the Jubilee, you know the interested people started to notice things then ....

While there is a frank acknowledgment on the part of certain participants that the monarchy is not of great interest to young people, some of them draw a connection between the failure to assimilate to an assumed set of conventional anglo-conformist values and a dislike of the monarchy. Through the rhetorical use of deixis and, in particular, pronouns, Bill draws a distinction between us and them. In so doing, Bill is making a core claim for the superiority of these values and their status as definitive of the established culture. Bill argues:

> It [monarchy] appeals a lot to the older crowd, the older generation that feel allegiance there, but—I listen to a lot of talk radio—there are a lot of people that are against the monarchy [that] come from other countries that are opposed to the Crown and opposed to everything it really stands for, and you know instead of coming to Canada and realizing what we have here, they bring their issues here and then try to get rid of anything that represents what they dislike, which includes the Queen.

When it comes to the Oath of Citizenship, many Orangemen take a hard line on any objections to swearing allegiance to the Queen. Art puts it this way, again as if in an address to a prospective new immigrant, expressing his resolve both through the use of the imperative voice and through repetition:

> Well, like for swearing allegiance to the Queen, you know what you're going to be doing when you come here, you want to get your Canadian citizenship, you know what you're going to have to do. Hey, if you don't want to swear allegiance to the Queen, don't come over here, okay? If you don't want to swear allegiance to the Queen, don't bother coming over here, it's as simple as that.

The same viewpoint is expressed by Dave, who includes an implicit threat: "... so why would they stand up and say well, I want to be a Canadian citizen, but I don't want to swear allegiance to the Queen. Then don't be a Canadian citizen, that's up to you. If anything ever happens here and you break the law, they can send you back to where you came from … because you're not a Canadian." Representing a less hard-line and more traditionally conservative paternalistic, accommodationist, and ameliorative perspective, which includes both a support for multiculturalism and a clear understanding of the centrality of the Crown in the Canadian Constitution, Mike offers the following reasoning regarding the future of the monarchy in Canada:

> Canada of course, it's a country in flux. Immigration form countries that would support the monarchy is nil. Immigration from countries that have no idea what the monarchy is, are the ones that we're seeing coming into this country and that's fair enough. I'm not discriminating between who should come and who shouldn't. It's just that I don't think our government does enough, you know, to illustrate what the monarchy means, other than that they get a small folded book to look through—you have to tell us how many provinces there are in Canada and you have to nanananana [sic]—so you pass this quasi-test of some kind and you stand up and take your oath and "I do solemnly promise that I will support and maintain the Queen and all her consorts as long as he or they shall; support and maintain the Protestant faith"—so, it's under threat because over time the support for the monarchy, it's wavering. It's still quite strong and even if it were to come to a point where they would try to get rid of it, it would require the co-operation of each Provincial jurisdiction in Canada.

The relationship between indigenous Canadians and the Crown is complex, and such complexity is reflected in the perspectives of Canadian Orangemen. On the one hand, the Orange Order celebrates an unselfconscious anglo-normative coloniality and white settler values. On the other hand, Orangemen are aware of the long-standing fiduciary relations that were established between the Crown and indigenous peoples in the Royal Proclamation of 1763, and other historical bonds. Those indigenous Canadians who worked and fought alongside the British in North America themselves became members of Orange Lodges, such as the Mohawk Lodge of the Tyendinaga Reserve. Among the more prominent indigenous Orangemen was Dr. Oronhyatekha (1841–1907), who was a Mohawk physician, scholar, Oxford scholar, and confidant of Prime Ministers Sir John A. Macdonald and Sir Wilfrid Laurier (Montanini 2017). The general orientation toward indigenous people among contemporary Orangemen is one of respect. Harold says:

> They [indigenous people] claim to be loyal to the Queen … they are … Yeh, they had a lot of Orange lodges … I've talked to guys in the s World War and they've fought with—they had aboriginals, Indians like for scouts and that, and they said they were great soldiers, and very loyal. First and Second World War, you know? Yea. All I ever heard from veterans—talk to them—was good things about them [indigenous peoples].

The basis for support for the monarchy is a variant of tribal loyalty. The degree of in-group endogamy is less pronounced in Canada than it is in Northern Ireland. The boundaries of group belonging and of community distinctiveness are far less pronounced in the Canadian context. However, even in Canada, there is a clear sense of loyalty surrounding the affirmation of the Crown. There is a uniform belief that newcomers to Canada should pledge allegiance to the Queen. Art is only one of a number of Orangemen to criticize the periodic attempts to remove the pledge of allegiance to the Queen from citizenship ceremonies. He is concerned at the increasing numbers of people who do not want to swear allegiance to the Queen. While they do not regard it as a large constituency, both Clive and Dave make reference to those who protest against the Queen on Victoria Day weekend and in comments made on talk radio. Pete brings his reading of Canadian history and current affairs into a robust defense of the monarchy and in so doing articulates a certain view of Canada that conforms to the Orange experience:

> … it [the requirement in citizenship ceremonies that new Canadians swear allegiance to the Queen] was challenged recently and failed. It was actually challenged by an Irish Catholic, whose father was an IRA man, a Jamaican, Rastfarian, and a Jew, Jewish fellow. It was three of them—that was who challenged … this motion [sic] … I think it's a failure because if we allow it to go through, it attacks our identity, it attacks our history. Canada, Canadians have such a little amount of history … that the one thing that we do hold close is that—yes—we snuffed the Americans when they crossed that border. That's a big win for the Canadians. The Americans, the big beast to the South … the world power. Few countries can say "Yeh, we beat the world power."

With regard to the singing of the Royal Anthem, Pete says:

> I think that you shouldn't have to do it [sing "God Save the Queen"] every day, but I think it should be taught. It used to be in the schools. I think you should have it for Remembrance Day because Remembrance

Day we were serving our Queen. Our people were serving our Queen. Our country was serving our Queen.... There's a lot of Orangemen that feel very strongly about God Save the Queen coming back, 'cos it's played here at Remembrance Day, but it's not played in school on Remembrance Day, not necessarily, but a lot of them do though ... and when I was in school—I went to a Catholic school—and we did have God Save the Queen for the first part, and then they got rid of it over the years. It was a lot of the parents who were more of the republican nature didn't like it.

Harold also recalls singing God Save the Queen at school: "I went to public school and every morning the bible was out and the Lord's Prayer was said and we all sang God Save the Queen." Tom has vivid memories of the consequences of not standing up for the Queen, as well as a perspective on current Canadian standards of singing the Royal Anthem:

...once somebody got punched out in a theatre because they refused to stand up to sing The Queen ... after the movie. This was in the 1960s ... I very much believe that The Queen, the song, whatever the anthem, has a place in ceremonial situations ... I just wish that adults would sing it with more worth rather than the pathetic mewings that you get.

While there is generalized support for the singing of the Royal Anthem, Mike is clear that Canadian protocol places the Canadian national anthem first in precedence, above that of the Royal Anthem. Expanding upon the concept of shared, even divided, loyalties in the British Protestant diaspora, he unfolds a personal narrative:

Singing the ... Royal Anthem ... if it's going to be sung, it should always be sung following the national anthem. In our [Orange] meetings, we used to sing the national anthem at the opening of it, and God Save the Queen at the ending of the meeting.... Let me put it into perspective for you. I am a Canadian by choice rather than by definition. My country that bred me is still the place that I was born and always will have a place in my heart and my head and my body. But I came to this country because I wanted to be a part of it, and became a Canadian. So, for me the national anthem takes priority over the Royal Anthem. But It's not to say that the Royal Anthem—it should always be sung at any opportunity.

There is a core loyalty to the Crown and enthusiastic support for the monarchy among the participants. However, beyond the ritual of swearing and singing, as well as occasional interest in a royal visit, there is little direct attachment. Loyalty does, however, become amplified around questions of national belonging, which we also examine in the next chapter.

As we have seen, some Orangemen express a lamentation that Canadians are diminishing in their support for and loyalty to the monarchy. They do not detect a particular groundswell of opposition toward the monarchy, just a generalized indifference, fueled in part by immigration and multiculturalism, which is adding people to Canada with no royal traditions. Many of the Orangemen note that the French in Canada and Quebeckers, in particular, are the least supportive of the monarchy. As with many of their contemporaries in Canada and beyond, however, some of them make reference to the personal attributes of royal personages, such as Prince Charles, and argue that the British/Canadian royal family will increasingly be required to "Europeanize" and to cut back on the trappings of pomp and privilege. Tom explores what he perceives as the apathy of his fellow citizens regarding the monarchy:

> I don't think that most of (my fellow citizens) care one way or another ... I'm just going from my own experience, where I worked. I was about the only person that emphasized that we had to have a picture of the Queen, we had to have a picture, or the flag flying and things like that. The rest of them, they couldn't care less.

This perspective is shared by Clive, who argues that a decline in support for the monarchy is also a factor in the UK. The Orangemen share a generalized perspective that in order to survive, the monarchy will need to adapt. This is a version of the postmodern monarchy that is objectively antithetical to the traditional conservative origins of Orangeism. The traditional authority of the monarchy is grounded in hereditary lineage and an unquestioned fealty to the role, irrespective of any personal characteristics. Obedience is inherent in the role of subject, and the relationship between monarch and subject is enchanted, non-transactional, unconditional, and independent of any affective bonds. This traditional view is inherent in Art's claim that: "It shouldn't really matter who fills the role of King or Queen." Even though he shares popular misgivings about Prince Charles, Dave admits: "...but if Charles is going to be King, we'd still sing God Save the King." By way of contrast, the postmodern monarchy is disenchanted, personalized, contingent, transactional, and conditioned by affect. Mike sets the scene for the contemporary role of the monarchy in Canada:

Thirty to forty years ago, your loyalty to the monarchy was absolute. It was an expectation, and you testified to that in a certain oath every time you had a meeting, and that was put upon you. But today that's still put upon you, but you know if you were to look at monarchies all over Europe, you can see what's happening. They're all coming down to the grass roots level. They're all trying to relate to the person who's walking up and down the street and paying for them to do the things they do. And in a sense, our Queen has—she's done the same thing.

The high degree of personalization of the monarchy, and the contingency of its popularity, is expressed by Pete, who sketches over some contemporary UK history, assuming a common understanding of the royal sagas:

The Queen has become a bit of a rock star recently. I mean with the whole Olympics and everything else, I've found we've had a resurgence in support of the Queen. Diana was a very low point and in recent years as she's gotten older, she still keeps doing the job. It's [her popularity] gone up. So I would say—you know—no republican here is going to win that case at this point—not even close—not right now as long as Queen Elizabeth is still on the throne ... even the republicans came out and said "well, we wouldn't get rid of the monarchy until Queen Elizabeth left." They're too afraid to touch her because she's too much of a rock star around here.... I think Charles will be eighty. I think he'll be so bloody old by the time he gets it—if he takes it—'cos he might not even want to take it—as an eighty year old man I don't think I'm going to want to take—Queen Elizabeth, if she lives like her mother, she could be a hundred or more—he could be eighty years old by the time he ever gets to that throne. I tell you, I'm not wanting to be working past sixty-five, so I certainly don't want to be working when I'm eighty, right? So, he might just give it to his son, realizing that he's a lot more popular, 'cos his son is very popular—beautiful wife—very dashing—he's got—he's not wild like his brother—and he's a lot like his grandmother, which is good for that job. That's what you're going to need. You don't need anyone who's a rabble rouser, especially today where the media's on you [clicks fingers for emphasis] like that, especially British media.

Echoing these ideas, Dave notes that: "William and Kate are much loved, even in this country ... because they're a modern couple and because they're on the TV." Both Dave and Art also believe that Charles is less popular than the other royals, and that he has lost the respect of many people through his conduct. Dave says: "If Charles takes over, the interest—I don't think—would be the same, right? How can he be a King of England people have said. He's just married a divorced woman… It's sad, but I believe a lot of people would say don't make him King." Art says: "I think he's [Prince Charles] lost a bit of respectability …. They'd probably wait for William and Kate to get in there."

The Orangemen we spoke to were all monarchists and expressed an ongoing commitment to the Crown in the face of what they saw as waning Canadian support for and loyalty to the monarchy. At best, they sense a broad indifference to the Crown, which has come about through a changing Canada. Factors such as immigration and multiculturalism have added to a society with much weakened or no royal traditions. Orangemen still perceive, with some concern, the specter of the French in Canada and Quebeckers, who remain unsupportive, if not hostile to the monarchy. The British connection, through the monarchy and the Crown, is understood within Orangeism to be the pre-requisite of a stable society, but importantly for members, this is seen to be the Canadian Crown as discrete from the British Crown. As with their perceptions of the monarchy and the Crown, the beliefs and values that Canadian Orangemen hold vis-à-vis the State, political life, and policy, which we investigate in Chap. 5, make reference to former glories, lost opportunities, and fading influence. If the Crown survives mainly as a postmodern monarchy, the realm of the State and institutions of power and influence exhibit for many contemporary Canadian Orangemen characteristics that Beck et al. (1994) refer to those of "zombie institutions."

References

Beck, Ulrich, Anthony Giddens & Scott Lash. *Reflexive Modernization: Politics, Tradition and Aesthetics in the Modern Social Order*. Stanford: Stanford University Press, 1994.

Buckner, Phillip. "Introduction." In *Canada and the End of Empire*, edited by Phillip Buckner, 1–14. Vancouver: University of British Columbia Press, 2005.

Champion, C.P. *The Strange Demise of British Canada: The Liberals and Canadian Nationalism, 1964–1968*. Kingston: McGill-Queen's University Press, 2010.

Grand Orange Lodge of Ontario West. *Report of Proceedings of the 152nd Annual Sessions of the Right Worshipful Provincial Grand Lodge of Ontario West*. Niagara Falls. April 28–30th 2011. Unpublished.

Gray, Charlotte. "Reign Maker." *The Walrus*, January/February, 2012. http://walrusmagazine.com/articles/2012.01-politics-reign-maker/ Accessed 14 April, 2016.

Hillmer, Norman & Chapnick, Adam. "An Abundance of Nationalisms." In *Canadas of the Mind: The Making and Unmaking of Canadian Nationalisms in the Twentieth Century*, edited by N. Hillmer and A. Chapnick,3–14. Kingston: McGill-Queen's University Press, 2007.

Ibbitson, John. "The Remaking of the Canadian Myth." *The Globe and Mail*, May 2, 2012, A10. http://search.proquest.com/docview/1688076145/fulltextPDF/B07D3A48EE544103PQ/1?accountid=15115. Accessed 13 June, 2017.

Montanini, Chris. "Meet Dr. O, London's First Indigenous Physician". *London Free Press*, March 9, 2017. http://www.thelondoner.ca/2017/03/09/meet-dr-o-londons-first-indigenous-physician. Accessed May 1, 2017.

Nesbitt-Larking, Paul & James W. McAuley. "Securitization through Re-Enchantment: The Strategic Uses of Myth and Memory." *Postcolonial Studies*. Forthcoming.

Smith, Allan. *Canada An American Nation? Essays on Continentalism, Identity, and the Canadian Frame of Mind*. Kingston: McGill Queen's University Press, 1994.

Volkan, Vamik. "Psychoanalysis and Diplomacy: Part 1. Individual and Large Group Identity." *Journal of Applied Psychoanalytic Studies* 1.1. (2001): 29–55.

CHAPTER 5

The State

Abstract This chapter combines an analysis of Canadian Orange Order responses to the Canadian regime and government with a range of public policy issues. McAuley and Nesbitt-Larking undertake an analysis of the views of contemporary Canadian Orangemen on the Constitution, government, governance, political life, and public policy issues, including immigration, the French fact in Canada, bilingualism, and sexual politics. This chapter further investigates the complex relationship with Northern Irish politics and society, the uses of history, and the politics of memory in the construction of Canadian Orange identity.

Keywords The State · Government · Gender policy · Sexual politics Immigration · Bilingualism

Despite its claims to be only a religious organization, the Orange Order in Canada has always had a distinct political focus and role. As we have seen already, Orangeism first arrived in Upper Canada during the first few decades of the nineteenth century. It expanded rapidly, aided initially by British army personnel and then by migrating Irish Protestants bringing institutions with them or joining what was familiar from their homeland. It was strengthened through further waves of migration and by those joining because it had adapted itself to the local demands and conditions of a rapidly expanding society. The politics of welfare featured early, as the Order quickly developed to provide mutual support in order to take care of the sick and elderly.

By the early 1880s, the Order had established a pension and insurance scheme to raise money for the widows and orphans of deceased brethren. Today, Orange insurance still plays an important role in Canadian Orange ranks, but has expanded to serve all strata of Canadian society. Thus, for many, the Orange Lodges provided the only source of organized social welfare and served to ease some of the burdens of emigration and social hardship. Being a member of the Order carried clear and tangible benefits. Members received companionship, and more especially access to health insurance and burial funds, alongside building useful networks in the new society (MacRaild 2003/2004).

As we have stated, the Orange Order reached a peak in the early part of the twentieth century with almost 2500 lodges across Canada. Nowhere was its success, in terms of numbers of members, lodges, and political influence, more evident than in central and western Ontario. Operating predominately with an ethos of loyalty to Britain and being overwhelmingly Protestant, Ontario was, for Orangeism, worryingly wedged between the malign influences of the republican USA and Catholic Quebec. It thus developed a mind-set that was tailored by Orange ideology (Houston and Smyth 1984: 197) and structured by historical reference to, and memory of, the Siege of Derry. Canadian Orangemen too saw themselves as beset on all sides by enemies, both real and perceived. Hence, Orange identity was forged within this mentality and defined in opposition to American republicanism and the Catholicism of French Canada.

This sense of an identifiable Other helped create group coherence and cohesiveness, and the resulting networked strength of the in-group, echoed so strongly within local society that the Order came to achieve a position of power and respectability. It was able to attract thousands of non-Irish into its ranks, attracted by the core themes projected by the Order, of Protestantism and loyalty to the British connection (Walker 2007). Such values were widespread at this time and were far from exclusive to Irish Protestants. Orangeism appealed to swathes of the Canadian population, and the Order welcomed into its ranks not only English and Scottish migrants but also German Protestants, native-born Canadians, and even First Nations people (Kaufmann 1997).

The church continued to serve an important function in the formation of the cultural and social identity of Protestant emigrants. Alongside this, the Orange Order acted in part as a multiethnic defender of Loyalist Protestant Canada (Houston and Smyth 1980: 95–96). The Order was so successful that by the end of the nineteenth century, around one-third of all English-speaking Canadians were members (McAuley 1992). With this of course came a particular political worldview, committed to the defense of British North America which, although altered in context, remains deeply located in the minds of many contemporary Orangemen in Canada.

Orangeism was, and remains, rooted in religion (see Chap. 3) but its links to politics and the political are undeniable. From the beginning, it connected men, institutionally and ideologically, and linked them to a transnational political community that stretched far beyond the borders of North America (Harland-Jacobs 2008). The Grand Orange Lodge of Canada, established by the early 1830s, played a significant role in the political direction and social structure of the country. Its structure mirrored that found in Ireland. In creating guidelines and conventions for life in the New World, Orangemen adapted what they knew to have worked in the Old World. They drew on familiar organizational structures, practices, and protocols, and their primary reference points were those of Protestantism, loyalty, and conservatism, just as they had been in Ireland. They sought to ensure that Canada would be both British and Protestant, under the authority of the King (or Queen) and ultimately God (Houston and Smyth 1990: 181). As Houston and Smyth (1980: 185) express it:

> Orangeism and Irishmen were especially suited to British North America, for a society was being created there in the image of a British colony, not an independent separate state. Britain's first colony had been Ireland, and out of that tradition of colonial connection Orangeism had emerged.

Anglo-Britishness became a dominant feature of Canadian life, and the British historical narrative was used to counter the growing influence of the USA (Kaufmann 1997). For many Protestants at the time, a core feature of their social identity was to see themselves in the role of defenders of British Canada. Initially, the perceived threats were from the republic of the USA, but an internal threat was also detected in the shape of political agitation from French Canadians and nationalists. The Orange Order in response functioned to provide a direct link with the social and political values from across the Atlantic and to facilitate its transplantation and growth in its new surroundings.

The Orange Order in Ontario grew to be highly influential and was extensive in its social networks that reached into almost all facets of daily life. The Order was not only active in everyday politics but it also cultivated and fostered close links with many municipal and provincial politicians, mainly conservatives. As in Ireland itself, Orange membership was, in many cases, a necessary pre-requisite to find work opportunities and employment (McAuley 1992). Orangeism became an important political force in governing Toronto, manifest in its control of local patronage and, importantly, ensuring that this function was self-perpetuating. As Gavin recalls: "... you know you couldn't be—you couldn't be Mayor of Toronto unless were an Orangeman." Members enjoyed preferential access to networks that held considerable sway over the Canadian government and economy. In Toronto, the Orange Lodge was central to the making of personal relationships and deals among the city's growing business classes in the late nineteenth century. As Jenkins (2003: 82) explains, it was the Order that: "embedded Protestant identities and provided access to social networks", which in turn could then be: "converted to power within both the labour market and apparatuses of government (local, provincial, federal)." City Officials, for example, were almost always Orange members, and the Orange approved slate proved crucial in election results. Patronage was widespread and extensive, as Dave reveals:

> [The Orange Order] used to be a very important part of it, especially in Ontario but not only in Ontario—right across our whole country even in Quebec—they've played a major role—Orangeism has played a major role ... well you couldn't get a job in the Toronto council if you weren't an Orangeman ... never mind being a Protestant.

As Fitzpatrick (1989) puts it, Toronto: "until the middle of the twentieth century was controlled, though by no means exclusively populated, by the Scots-Irish." The Order's influence was paramount and the effects could be readily found in both Toronto City Council and at Queen's Park, where they enforced both sabbatarianism and temperance, helping the city earn the character of "Toronto the Good." Indeed, it was not until the 1930s that the City of Toronto acquired its first non-Orange councilor. But the Order's power also extended beyond the city. Gavin explained:

> At one time you couldn't be Reeve of [named] Township if you didn't belong to an Orange Lodge. And I know when the first councilor [who wasn't an Orangeman] made it—it's not too many years ago. And he was going to be Reeve and he was running ... for most of his lifetime. I mean he was a real good guy ... but a couple of guys that were deep Orangemen made sure he didn't <u>make</u> it. [our emphasis] [laughs]

But it was in Toronto that the effects of the Orange slate were most profoundly felt. Most of Toronto's mayors throughout the nineteenth and early twentieth centuries belonged to the Order. According to Kaufmann (2007), the city had 30 Orange mayors in its history, and few non-Orangemen held the job until the late 1960s. William Dennison was the last Orangeman to hold the mayorship of Toronto in 1972. For a lengthy period, however, any level of political progress in the city was dependent upon the Order and guaranteed by lodge affiliation and support.

The Orders influence extended far beyond the parish pump or city politics, however, and reached as far as the Canadian Parliament. It supplied the country with four federal Prime Ministers and numerous provincial premiers, among them Ontario premiers, George Ferguson, from 1923 to 1930; George Henry, from 1930 to 1934; Thomas Kennedy, from 1948 to 1949; and Leslie Frost, from 1949 to 1961, were all Orangemen. The last Orange Prime Minister elected in Canada was Conservative John Diefenbaker in the 1960s.

Orangeism offered its members a religious-political identity that was transmitted and remained relevant on both sides of the Atlantic. The Order promoted a British way of life and opposed separatist nationalism, such as that found in French Quebec. This found expression at both the macro- and micro- levels of politics. Orangeism, for example, played a central role in the successful fight against Catholic school funding and other francophone-led causes in the late nineteenth century (Kaufmann 2004). Such actions were seen within the context of need to defend Protestantism and the ethnic link with Britain, and included particular political viewpoints, including support for the monarchy and largely conservative values. Religion provided a guide to political action and Canadian Orangeism attempted to preserve identity formations, based on religious observance, political allegiance, and modes of cultural representation.

Most Orangemen interviewed conveyed a direct or indirect reference to their British connections. British heritage is a strong part of their personal identity and often prompted individuals to join the Orange Order, and the roots of such beliefs lie deep. Indeed, part of the attraction of Orangeism for many was always its pro-empire, pro-Protestant focus, which initially appealed to new settlers in maintaining connections and expressing loyalty to the "old country." The Orange Order was transnational from its earliest days and established itself with varying degrees of success across Africa, the Americas, Austrasia, and Europe. Kaufmann (2007) notes that in Canada (and Australia), Orangeism was very much rooted in British-Protestant ethnicity that reproduced those hierarchies of power found in the imperial heartland. The British Crown and the Protestant faith were therefore central to transnational constructions of Orange Britishness.

Loyalty to Crown influenced many issues in Canada, and the decline of the British Empire emphasized the changed nature of local identity and relationships for many Orangemen, resulting in new expressions of national identity. But an inherent British dimension loitered on in debates around policy, among them metrication, official languages policy, and multiculturalism. Perhaps, the clearest example was in 1965 and the intense debate as to whether Canada should retain the Union Jack or adopt a new Maple Leaf symbol as its national flag. At the time, members of the Orange Order expressed strong opposition to the new flag. The notion of loyalty still manifests itself in ongoing arguments surrounding commemoration, especially the use of symbols and rituals, in the funding of public schooling and in the use of the Lord's Prayer in educational surroundings.

The Orange Order has a long record of involvement in Canadian politics, both in the macro-politics of party influence and structure, and importantly also in the politics of everyday life. The Order's direct political influence has of course faded. Indeed, the election of Dennison as mayor of Toronto may be thought of as a last hurrah for Orangeism in terms of formal politics. It must be said at this point that politics and underlying religious beliefs are not always easily separated in the minds of Orangemen. As Chap. 3 indicates, for many religion is not merely about ritualistic worship, but rather a guide to action in everyday life, and the resulting political perspectives are derivatives of that religion. Protestantism, social activity, and political outlooks are thus inseparable. So too is an awareness of their British heritage. Reference is often made to the British origins of Orangeism in Canada and the cultural and social values that flow from it. Moreover, that British heritage is often perceived to be under threat, besieged from a society that no longer respects its British connections and traditions as a constitutional monarchy. As Art put it:

> ... the threat is ... I think it's very real ... from what our culture is now to what is was even ten years ago I think—I think it's changed—it's not everything at one time, like they're not going to do away with [it] all in one go, it's brick by brick. You know we've lost scripture reading in school, we've lost the singing of our National Anthem in a lot of schools ... you know ... they don't pledge allegiance or anything like that anymore ... it's just slowly ... like all our values are slowly going.

The participants made repeated reference to the social opprobrium accorded to those who stand up for Christianity, or traditional values, such as loyalty to the Crown and State. For Roy, adherence to such attitudes brings consequences:

> I see the allegiance to the crown, or the way that we associate ourselves with the crown, the same way I see a—the same way as we associate ourselves with our brothers in Northern Ireland, you know I think that when the cry comes out that they need help, it's up to those of us in the colonies, to at least put our shoulder to the wheel a little bit because they have, that's a tough, that's a tough way to live.

Loyalty to the monarch and the Crown are seen by Orangemen as prerequisites of a stable society, but importantly it is also increasingly to the Canadian Crown as distinct from the British Crown. Broadly, most Orangemen we interviewed expressed some degree of pride in their history and heritage, with the Protestant Reformation and its associations with the rise of liberalism, democracy, and enlightened thinking. The centrality of protecting the civil rights and religious liberties of all, not just Protestants, was fairly prominent in their worldview. Jim explains:

> I'm very cognoscente [sic] of individual rights and, I think Protestantism over all gives more, leeway to the individual, over history, as far as being able to read and think different things, and you know, a lot of, a lot of our Western democracy and Liberal thought evolved from the Protestant Reformation.

Orangemen are fundamentally conservative in their ideological leanings and support both economic conservatism and social conservatism. They tend to vote for the Conservative Party (see Appendix B). According to George's views of his fellow Orangemen: "they're pretty well much right wing and free enterprise I'd say." Such views were largely reflected in Orangemen's links with formal politics. The Order's mainstream nature and its political reputation as a bastion of popular Toryism are attested to by the many politicians who passed through its ranks and the major voting patterns found within the history of the Order. According to Roy: "most Orangemen are right of centre on most things ... I would say the majority would be right of centre." As Mike explains, members were historically encouraged to vote: "Conservative ... whenever there was a national vote or a provincial vote it was—the expectation was that the Lodge would sort of fall in behind and vote for them." Keith sums up, broadly, where he thinks Orange Order members stand:

> I think by definition we tend to look very conservative still because of our mandate—like we're monarchists and we're up for law and order—we support our military in a really big way—so those are typically presumed in current society as—as conservative.

All three men were at pains to point out, however, this was the conservatives of the past. Mike articulated this as follows:

> I mean at one time the Lodge was probably always associated with the Conservative Party of Canada—that was the Conservative Party that's no longer with us—you know ... but it disappeared you know because political parties here as you're probably aware ... look so different today from the Conservatives of yesterday ... the Conservatives today are the NDP [New Democratic Party] or Liberals of 20 years ago. So they have moved their position and their spectrum of politics—you know the Conservative Party today occupies a space that right wing Liberals would typically have held.

Most of those interviewed placed themselves and fellow members on the right of the political spectrum. As Harold said: "In the lodge ... I don't think so, no, no ... no we haven't, there's no NDP in our lodge either, or even in this area." While George expressed his opposition to left-wing ideas and parties most forcibly when he said:

Well I think a lot of the NDP and a lot of the Liberals are communist, you know ... they may not belong to the Communist Party, but their views are all communist. I don't think they want free enterprise like you can go out and farm, have your own farm and do what you want or if you want to start up a business and do whatever you want, you know, invest money and take a chance on making a million, or losing a million, that's your own business, but I think they more or less wanted everything to be under the government control.

Where do Orange members stand on some of the major social issues of the day? We discussed homosexuality with them. While acknowledging a certain degree of awkwardness, many of the participants expressed a willingness to accept gay men into the Orange Order and some made note of the fact that a number already belong. On homosexuality, the following comments were typical, Keith said: "...like same sex marriage or homosexuality—really hot topics—we're far more liberal here [than in Northern Ireland]" and "we're far more tolerant of other cultures." While Mike said:

> If you ask me as a Canadian how do I feel about it, yeh it's very simple: if you are a homosexual, and you want to practice your modus operandi [sic] ... in the privacy of where I practice mine, being the bedroom ... then you're quite welcome to do that ... but just don't come out into the open and say "Hi I'm coming out and I expect more rights than anybody else."

Asked if a homosexual man would be allowed to join, or even be welcomed into the association, there was broad, if somewhat guarded, agreement. Roy's views were fairly typical, when he said: "I don't think they'd have any problem, you know it's like the, it's like the navy thing, uh, don't tell, don't show [don't ask, don't tell] ... And that was probably wise."

A minority were supportive of social policy that included same-sex marriage. Interestingly, Tom regarded himself as uncharacteristically liberal when he noted: "Well, personally the law of the land says they can get married. I don't have a problem with it, but I suspect I'm the only member (who thinks that), a minority of one." In fact, his views would have been supported by some others. Clive articulates the "no special privileges" viewpoint quite clearly in the following passage:

> That's one of the things within the Orange Order ... equal rights for everyone, special privileges for none ... special privileges for none. So you know I mean presumably then if a gay or homosexual guy wanted to join the Orange order that would probably be okay. Wouldn't have a problem. He might find it ... a bit of getting used to but I guess he would survive ... other things being equal ... if he was Protestant and a monarchist ... I believe that's what we would look at first ... what kind of a person is this? Is he in your face all the time? Telling you I want special rights ... no he wouldn't be welcome here ... not because you're homosexual or gay ... not because of that ... but because you're in everybody's face. Telling them that they're wrong and they want special rights and you'd feel you had to give them what they want.

While there is something of a pervasive discomfort with homosexuality, and a formal opposition toward the extension of gay rights in public policy, many participants express relatively tolerant, if rather brittle and restricted, views, and only a few adopt the hard-line of regarding homosexuality as a sin and "an abomination." Most Orangemen adopt a "live and let live" approach and believe that homosexual men would be accepted into the Orange Order provided they were good Orangemen, did not flaunt their lifestyle, and did not attempt to promote their ways of being. Mike expresses the ambivalence of the men toward homosexuality:

> I know this big debate in the Lodge when Canada enacted the Bill to allow gay marriage ... now the Orange Order, in principle, for the most part was against that ... but that was a funny thing because I think that was a generational thing too, because when I spoke against it, my son and daughter thought I was crazy.

Bill articulates the familiar line on gay rights that it is acceptable, provided the adherents do not flaunt their sexuality or make demands for special status:

> I think they [gay people] should have the same rights as anybody else. I mean, the law applies to everyone equally [but] I think what they're going for now is special rights. For whatever reason, you know maybe because my kids are in school now, I see it more. A lot of issues are all centred around gay rights, lesbian rights, bisexual rights. Bullying in particular. Bullying's always been an issue in school. For some reason now, they're

making it a gay issue. My youngest one, she's only 11, and she's already having that gay lifestyle taught to her and it's like—well, at 11, I didn't have that kind of thing pushed on me—either straight or gay ... under the law, they're [gay people] entitled to a job just like anybody else, they're entitled to be protected from attack from—for any reason, you know, whether it be because of their sexual preference, their religious faith, everyone has that protection under the law—so I don't think there's any need for special rights. Yeh, equal rights, yes, special rights, no.

Another feature of the interviews was the attitude expressed toward French Canada and its construction by Orangeism as "another place" in Canadian society. Tensions between French and English Canada are of course long-standing. They are brought into focus by loyalty as a keystone of Orange belief and the perceived obligations by members of the Order to defend Protestantism and the monarchy. Orangemen commonly express, at best, a wariness of French Canada, as unlikely to commit to these values and, at worst, a hostility to the constructs of French Canada.

Roy explained that Protestantism was under threat because: "Quebec runs Canadian politics." He spoke triumphantly of a small anglophone town in Quebec, a Protestant enclave, in which the locals had managed to keep Catholicism from spreading into their community and had cleverly deceived the Quebec state over regulations governing the presence of the French language in public places. Ostensibly pleased to permit the language bureaucrats to replace the English language public signage, the townspeople apparently proceeded to unscrew all the French signs and replace them with the original English ones shortly after cheerily waving goodbye to the French language agents.

He tells the story as follows:

> In [anglo town] Quebec, there are ... 11 or 12 Protestant churches, but being in Quebec you'd expect a Catholic church, there was no Catholic church in the county of [anglo], it's all Protestant. And when they come ... from Quebec City to change the signs, and put them in French, whoever the Mayor is goes out, helps the, the city fathers help, they take down all these English signs and they throw them in the dump, and then they get two busloads of people to go back to Quebec City, who've come from there. And the next day they go out to the dump, get all the signs and bring them back in and put them up, and from the highest point in [anglo town], flies a Union Jack. Always, 365 days a year....

Some of this reluctance to accept the politics of French Canada is long-standing. Within the narrative of the Order, French-Canadian Catholics have been regarded both as culturally backward and as politically subversive. There were a variety of views expressed following this line, Dave suggesting that: "French Canadians themselves are not loyal enough" and that "their sole purpose was to get out of Canada." Harold expressed views that were indicative:

> ...when Quebec wants to talk about separation, that worries me ... that really does worry me, about Quebec separating right? ... because that's going to divide Canada, like you know? and you know the, the history books, you know you go back to Wolfe. And you know, they had that battle there and there's only one thing they done wrong, they give the French a little bit of land, and they showed them, when they had them down the should have said you're out, either come with us or stay out ... but they give them that, they felt sorry for them, they give them that little bit of land and now they're getting bigger and bigger and bigger and bigger and they want to take part of the Canada away ... like I think Quebec's like, there's just a, it just takes one or two rotten apples to spoil the bag you know? And that's, that's what is there, just a couple people or a few people, they think oh, this, this, lets separate, separate you know?

Such concerns led Pete to consider the question of identity in broader terms and conclude:

> I think ... you have four different Canadas—you have English Canada, French Canada and you have immigrant Canada and of course you have native of course as well—but the native Canadian ... among English Canadians I think you still have great loyalty to the Queen—because there's a history there.

However, despite some circumspection regarding the politics and ultimate loyalty of Quebeckers, the Orangemen did show support for official bilingualism and in some cases even some enthusiasm. One talked with pride about his wife being fully bilingual and his daughter taking lessons in French immersion.

There is a great pride and deep support for the Canadian armed forces among the Orangemen. Alongside this runs a whole series of events of commemoration and memorialization that go to form the Orange calendar. In many ways, loyalty to the military is seen to act as a proxy for both the Crown and State. With some justification, those interviewed see the history of Canadian Orangemen as intertwined with that of the military. Certainly, Orangemen volunteered in numbers to express their commitment to Canada and the Crown as an integral part of British identity. The list of conflicts in Canadian history is reasonably long: the War of 1812, the rebellions of Upper and Lower Canada (1837); the 1866 Fenian Raids; the Riel Rebellions (1869–1870, 1885); the Manitoba Schools Question (1890); the Boer War (1899–1902); and the two World Wars of 1914–1918 and 1939–1945, when Orange halls throughout rural Canada were commonly used as recruiting centers. This history is reasonably well-known by Orangemen, here Keith gives his version:

> ...in the 19th century that really united Orangemen in the cause ... there was other ones, but three big ones ... the War of 1812, the 1837 rebellion and then the third one would be the Fenian raids mixed with the Red River rebellion—right? So those three things really got Orangemen together 'cos they won every one of them and that was some ... that was really important because one thing that unites Ulster Orangemen is that they won and they've survived ... and that's one of the things that they hold so dear so every time they think they're losing ... that's why they always reflect back on what they did ... that won ... so Canadian Orangemen always reflected back on all the stories of all the battles they won ... they won the War of 1812 and kept the Americans at bay; they won in the 1837 rebellion of Mackenzie King—[sic] Orangemen died in that and actually served ... there was no military ... there was no police ... so the Orangemen said ... you guys are the most organized group ... so take guns and put that down ... and they did ... battle of the windmill I think it was called.

Orangemen recall proudly the role that they played in such events. Dave says: "...in the War of 1812, people around from this area—which was all horse and buggy farmland and all—were Orangemen—of course people had volunteered in the First World War—were actually Orangemen." Or these events recalled by Ian: "Yea, July 1st 1916. Anniversary of the Battle of the Somme ... well you know all about the Newfoundland Regiment, eh? They were pretty well wiped out practically. All Orangemen." Then in the twentieth century, a series of military encounters set about defining the nation, and within this, the Battle of Vimy Ridge in 1917 is set as the essential moment delineating Orange honor and enormity of commitment. While the battle was a victory for the Canadians, they endured tens of thousands of losses, many of them young Orangemen. The loss of these lives is part of the narrative of Orangeism in Canada. It enters into Orange collective memory as part of that narration (Anderson 1983: 204). It provides the reason for dramatic drops in the ranks of Orange membership. Such events give rise to the notion that the Order would be much stronger than it is today and that the Order have suffered because sacrifice is firmly established. Pete expresses the matter this way:

> ...the wars killed us—the wars—you know after that the wars killed us—that was a loss to us—we lost whole lodges that were wiped out—because like you guys—you know city lodges—like city units—so a city would go into battle and would get wiped out and when they came back there was nobody left ... there's a lot of little towns like that and they got wiped out and that killed a lodge and that—the next war killed the lodge because they went in mass.

This perspective is supported by Art who says:

> ...we lost out because there were so many [killed] in the First World War? In the Second World War? We would have had like—a lot of those guys and maybe their sons joining [the Orange Order].

Clive argues that:

> Our numbers are so low now—like it's—the First World War really took away from the Orange because of the number of—Members that were killed—and again going into the Second World War, the volunteers from the Orange Lodges again was huge—and our Lodges just declined because of the number of people that were casualties.

Orangemen exhibit enormous gratification in the military and are highly protective of the armed forces. This also explains the emphasis placed by them on commemoration and memorialization. For Dave: "Veterans are a big part of not only this lodge, but I believe the Orange Order ... Veterans and Remembrance Day parades are a big part of us ... we've walked ... have done for many years and lay a wreath and all." This is of course not just Canadian history, but rather Orange Canadian history that is being constructed as a collective memory through which communities and groups represent their history to produce accounts of past events that shape the present.

Ireland is the spiritual and organizational home of Orangeism. Some of the men we interviewed were born there, many had parents who were born there, and most have relations there. It is a common focus for the men, but for some, it proved only of passing interest. Others see events as central, both in terms of what is happening with the Orange Order there and the general political circumstances. Most of the men tend to see it within a framework of Protestant versus Catholic relations, although others, particularly if they have emigrated from the Province of Northern Ireland, have adopted a rather more politicized framework. Indeed, one long-standing member, Phil, put his involvement with the Order directly down to his engagement with Northern Ireland:

> So like, it was true that a personal involvement though a personal touch that I became a member as well, 1970 ... I don't have to tell you what was happening at that time, I was very much a Canadian Unionist, so politically I was in line, politically speaking with what the Orange Lodge stood for at that time.

He continued:

> I guess you can go back and thank in part ... Bernadette Devlin for my being a member, because she came to North America and, in my opinion, spread a lot of mis-truths and it was all eaten up by American broadcasters, and then this is where I contend you know that the loyalist side at that time kind of lost the PR war ... and that was a factor ... because they didn't have anyone over here.

Gavin, for one, claimed that:

> I don't pay attention to 'em (events in Northern Ireland). I don't agree with them. I don't agree with condemning the Catholics like they do. I have my daughter-in-law's a Catholic and my—one of my nieces is. But they er—she's turned over—she's [long pause] what you call it a liberal Catholic.

For most, however, events in Northern Ireland are a regular topic of discussion. According to Art: "it is always there ... it's not part of the agenda, it's never discussed as an on the floor topic ... but we discuss it between ourselves—[we are] fairly aware of what is going on." While Bill describes the following situation: "You know we were quite aware of what's happening there and we do get correspondence from people there—So for our own interests we also like to know what going on." Understandably, the level of discussion and interest altered with the Troubles, according to Mike: "... in those times what you would find that discussion inside a Lodge meeting would certainly devote itself to a lot more of the things that were happening in Ulster ... than what was happening in Canada." He went on to point out:

> even recently you would have been talking about what was happening in Northern Ireland—oh yes always—because you had so many people in our Lodge—and that's the one I can speak for—that would go over there and come back, go over and come back and many of them still held membership in the Lodge they belonged to before they came to Canada.

Not that former membership in Northern Ireland was any guarantee that affiliation would be continued in Canada, as Ian puts it: "It's interesting to note that people who come here from Northern Ireland do not generally join the Lodge, and that's an interesting fact ... they don't because they don't see the need." Mike relates the following:

> ... you know, in business I ran into managers and people in—I sold industrial product, people in decision making who were from Northern Ireland ... I know they were Protestants and I asked them about joining the Orange Lodge here and they said no I had enough of that back home.

Nor did the situation in Northern Ireland encourage some to show their support in the way many members hoped. Roy reported a good example of this:

> I was talking to [Orange Order Official] ... we're coming back from a meeting and he said, you know ... every time there's a shooting in Northern Ireland we lose members in Canada, and I said why? What, he said because, he said, they're not into this violence thing.

On the other hand, there are those who are deeply involved in following what is happening, Pete saying of himself laughing: "the guys call me the propaganda minister ... I follow them [events in Northern Ireland?]

closely … because I'm that kind guy. I follow the events and I pass them around and we use Facebook as a as a medium." There are still close links to Northern Ireland, whether it be members returning home or visiting for the 12 July celebrations. Moreover, those that have been to Northern Ireland seem to have a higher status among peers than many others and are often deferred to in terms of their knowledge concerning such matters, often returning as they do with tales of involvement in the realities of Northern Ireland. The following is one example, as told by Ian:

> I have one of the rubber bullets that the … this one time the British soldiers was firing on the, on the Protestants, right down on Mersey Street, and [named person] was standing with his door open, and there was a rubber bullet came down, bouncin' down Mersey and stuck his foot out, and hit his foot and bounced into the, right to his step and I have it. He gave it to me, I have it at home.

When asked to compare membership of the Orange Order in the two jurisdictions, Bill answered as follows:

> Well, [in Northern Ireland] you could go out in … and end up in jail … you know, here you go out with your family and you have a good day … a perfect day … over home you just can't. I always say you look behind you and see what's coming … you know … and er to me that's the biggest difference. You're not going to run into guys that are ready to take your heads off and stuff like that here. It's more social over here … back home it's not. There's not as many social functions … we would run dances … family days … back home that doesn't happen.

Recognizing this, Roy points to one of the essential differences:

> See they see the need in Northern Ireland for protection, and, and, and they do it for protection, and they don't do it here for that reason, because their neighbor is a Roman Catholic, or the person they work with is a Roman Catholic, or maybe, you know, their boss, whatever. And so they, well, say well it's a different thing here, we can get along with Roman Catholics here, they don't pose a threat.

While Mike points out: "People coming over from Northern Ireland often express surprise about the differences here … it's on a smaller scale … I think they also like, the very casual attitude at which we all are together."

Jim speaks for many in the Order when he says: "the whole idea with the differences between the Orange Association in Canada and the Orange Association in Ireland, is they have a vested and viable purpose for being there because their neighborhoods are threatened in many instances."

The lives of Canadian Orangemen are distinctly bland and mundane. There are few of the great highs and lows or major political events that have accompanied the fate of the Orange Order in Northern Ireland. It is to be expected that many of their chosen traumas and glories (Volkan 2001) are borrowed, to the extent that they exist at all. The construction of meta-narratives is made easier through the availability of social representations that are definitive, dramatic, and dynamic. A number of Canadian Orange participants invoke borrowed collective memories of the Northern Irish Troubles and refer to people they have known who were embroiled in that far-away violence, thereby forging bonds of brotherhood across the Atlantic Ocean.

The Orange Order in Canada is avowedly apolitical and does not seek political office. Yet, as is apparent from the above, the membership holds clear and strong positions, and as a group are largely conservative politically, albeit with a small "c". So how do members feel that they can make such views relevant and what political weight do members feel they can exert. Mike says this concerning the politics of Orangeism:

> The Lodge—Orange Lodge in Canada-could have become a political force, back probably around the 1920s, when the numbers were ascending, and they had people in the federal government, we had prime ministers, we had members of parliament, we had mayors, we had—you know—in those days if the Lodge had wanted to turn itself into a political force it could have been one. But it didn't—it concentrated on its roots and its core values of faith, monarchy, you know role of government, all the things that the order still stands on today.

But in a remarkably honest assessment of where the Order stands today, Jim says:

> How relevant are we? Not much ... simply because our numbers are not enough to make an influence on decision making processes anywhere, we couldn't, if we were to take every Orangemen that exists in Canada and put them in one riding for a City Election, for a Municipal Election, we could not elect a member, we could not elect a councilor, and yet our membership across the board still believes we are a political force in

Canada. The reality is we are not, we once were, today we are not, but our opinions can influence decisions depending on where you sit and meet, but not, not overall but generally.

Dave gives one example of their failure to exert any political pressure:

> We recently wrote a letter to a [named] city council ... about the Lord's Prayer, right—we just got the word that ... somebody had sat in council meetings and objected to them saying the Lord's Prayer ... and they said it had gone to the Supreme Court and they had won their case ... it didn't go to any Supreme Court, the council decided. So there was a bit of a fear, so I wrote to [the council] and I also wrote to the provincial government because it was thought then that they were going to stop the Speaker saying the Lord's Prayer.

This was of fundamental concern to Orangemen and seen as an attack on key principles:

> I tell you what I decided to do to—let's go down I said in the Rangers Club—and I said and—come on and we'll protest at Queen's Park and Saturday morning because they're going to—[other members said] are you daft? You're daft!! Whereas other people are organized We can't organize like that no more.

It is indicative of the state of the organization that the attempt to organize a protest, even on a fundamental issue like this one, was met with such a reaction. As Clive puts it: "I mean should it be doing more to try and be heard? ... except there's nobody listening to the Orange Order any more ... I don't know what influence we have and—I don't think they have anybody strong enough to stand up for us." Irrespective of Clive's concerns regarding the present structure of leadership and authority within the contemporary Orange Order in Canada, there is, for many, the solace of the past, and of remembered and memorialized prominence and influence.

During a research visit on a guided tour of a Canadian Orange hall, a local lodge convenor spoke to us with pride and detailed knowledge about the history of the Orange Order in Canada, invoking the dominant discourses of Orangeism in a series of comments, and projected a guardedly optimistic view regarding the future of the Order. The convenor detailed the huge influence and pervasiveness of the Orange Order in nineteenth-century Ontario and made reference to a series of heroic Orangemen of the past, including military heroes. There were also villains, including the French and Catholic Métis leader of the nineteenth century, Louis Riel, who in 1870 ordered the execution of Orangemen Thomas Scott. Referring to the recent attempts to restore Riel to the status of a national hero, the convenor asserted "over our dead bodies."

All of these stories of the past drew the selective and partial uses of collective memory, chosen traumas and glories. Such memories can be specific to generations, or groups of people born and living during approximately the same period (Misztal 2003; Connerton 1989). Members of the same generation are part of the same historical and social circumstances, and these affect what, and how, different generations remember (Eyerman 2011).

Orangemen speak fondly of the great parades of the past, when there was no doubt as to the power and the glory of Orangeism. There were decades when the Orange Order constituted a vibrant and active community, when people bought their houses to be close to the Orange hall and when you could not get a job as a policeman or a fireman if you were not a member. But to be effective, collective memories must also speak to the present and the future, and carry meaning in contemporary society. It is here that the Orange Order has faced its greatest struggle. As with any fading organization, there are urgent disputes about what to do and what are the priorities in terms of social and political perceptions. There is individual engagement with issues of social and political concern, but at the moment, they exist without a vibrant or continuing mandate or sense of direction. The results are a kind of lamentation regarding former glories and a sad resignation about the fate of the Orange Order, at least in so far as political activism and political involvement is concerned. Despite this, the organization continues and the core values live on. What is the nature of the small community that preserves and promotes this heritage, and in so doing sustains a climate of hope while keeping the faith? This is the focus of Chap. 6, our final substantive chapter.

References

Anderson, Perry. *Imagined Communities: Reflections on the Origin and Spread of Nationalism*. London: Verso, 1983.

Connerton, P. *How Societies Remember*. Cambridge: Cambridge University Press, 1989.

Eyerman, R. 'The Past in the Present: Culture and the Transmission of Identity' in *The Collective Memories Reader*, edited by J. K. Olick, V. Vinitzky-Seroussi, and D. Levy, Oxford: Oxford University Press, 2011.

Fitzpatrick, Rory. *God's Frontiersmen: The Scots-Irish Epic*. London: Wiedenfeld and Nicolson, 1989.

Harland-Jacobs, Jessica. "Maintaining the Connection: Orangeism in the British North Atlantic World, 1795–1844." *Atlantic Studies* 5.1. (2008): 27–49.

Houston, Cecil J. and William J. Smyth. *The Sash Canada Wore: A Historical Geography of the Orange Order in Canada*. Toronto: University of Toronto Press, 1980.

———. "Transferred Loyalties: Orangeism in the United States and Ontario." *American Review of Canadian Studies* 14.2. (1984): 193–211.

———. *Irish Emigration and Canadian Settlement: Patterns, Links, and Letters*. Toronto: University of Toronto Press, 1990.

Jenkins, William. "Between the Lodge and the Meeting House: Mapping Irish Protestant Identities and Social Worlds in Late Victorian Toronto." *Social and Cultural Geography* 4.1. (2003): 75–98.

Kaufmann, Eric. "Condemned to Rootlessness: The Loyalist Origins of Canada's Identity Crisis." *Nationalism and Ethnic Politics* 3.1. (1997): 110–136.

———. "The Decline of the WASP in the United States and Canada." In *Rethinking Ethnicity: Majority Groups and Dominant Minorities*, edited by Eric Kaufmann, 61–83. London: Routledge, 2004.

———. "The Orange Order in Ontario, Newfoundland, Scotland and Northern Ireland: A Macro-social Analysis." In *The Orange Order in Canada*, edited by D.A. Wilson, 42–68. Four Courts Press: Dublin, 2007.

MacRaild, Donald M. "Wherever Orange Is Worn: The Orange Order and Irish Migration in the 19th and Early 20th Centuries." *The Canadian Journal of Irish Studies* 28.2.–29.1. (2003/4): 98–117.

McAuley, James W. "Under an Orange Banner: Reflections on the Northern Protestant Experiences of Immigration." In *The Irish Worldwide: History, Heritage, and Identity*, edited by Patrick O'Sullivan, 43–69. Leicester: Leicester University Press, 1992.

Misztal, B. *Theories of Social Remembering*. Maidenhead: Open University Press, 2003.

Volkan, Vamik. "Psychoanalysis and Diplomacy: Part 1. Individual and Large Group Identity." *Journal of Applied Psychoanalytic Studies* 1.1. (2001): 29–55.

Walker, Brian. "'The Lost Tribes of Ireland': Diversity, Identity and Loss Among the Irish Diaspora." *Irish Studies Review* 15.3. (2007): 267–282.

CHAPTER 6

Community

Abstract The final substantive chapter, concerns "Community." Included in this chapter are accounts of the views of contemporary Canadian Orangemen on gender, in-group solidarity, community outreach, parades and marching, and respectability. McAuley and Nesbitt-Larking explore these themes throughout this chapter and address four inter-related questions of the community for today's Canadian Orangemen. First, where have they come from? What are their traditions and their roots? Second, who are they? What is their community, and how do they sustain their values and solidarity among themselves? Third, where are they going? How open are they toward others, and are they recruiting younger members? Finally, how do they tell their story? How do they communicate their message to others within and beyond the Orange Order?

Keywords Community · Gender · Parades · Conviviality · Charity Recruitment

Following the work of McMillan and Chavis, McAuley (2016) says:

> ...there are four core elements in understanding community. Membership is experienced through: shared feelings of belonging and personal connection; through a sense that it makes a difference being part of a particular group; the belief that the physical and emotional needs of members are

best met through the benefits that group membership brings; and, by way of shared feelings of connection, and commitment to the belief that members have a shared common history, sense of place, experience and identity. (McAuley 2016: 76)

We explore these themes throughout this chapter and address four interrelated questions of the community for today's Canadian Orangemen. First, where have they come from? What are their traditions, their heritage, and their roots? Second, who are they? What is their community, and how do they sustain their values, their integrity, and solidarity among themselves? Third, where are they going? How open are they toward others? Are they recruiting and replacing their ranks with younger members? Are they relevant? Finally, how do they tell their story? How do they relate to non-members in their communities? How do they communicate their message to others?

There is a strong and pervasive sense of pride and dignity among the Orangemen we encountered in the course of our research, and a deep commitment to a shared heritage and tradition. Clive refers to an imagined past of omnipresence of the Orange Order across Ontario. However, his claim regarding the ubiquity of Orange halls is more than mere hyperbole and is supported by Kaufmann's (2007) historical research into the Ontario Orange Order at its height. This is reinforced by Clive who recalls:

> They said at one point in Ontario, you couldn't go more than 20 miles in any direction without coming on an Orange Lodge, an Orange hall. That's the way farmers worked, you know with moonlight. Worked in the full moon, and the distance between one hall and the other hall, that was as far as they went.

The importance of the Orange hall as a center of community, caring, and social activity is clearly evident among our participants. Trevor relates his introduction to the Orange community:

> My mother took me to this European supper, and there was some gentlemen there wearing their orange hats and wearing their orange sashes and collars, and they were kind of mingling around. And I asked my mother who they were, and she said "Well, they're a bunch of Orangemen." Well okay, and I never heard too much more about them.

Continuing with his narrative, Trevor explains how he came to join and to continue to value the Orange hall, expressing its importance to the life of the community and lamenting the loss of heritage and historical memory which comes with its disappearance. As with other Canadian Orangemen, Trevor's explanation for the decline of membership in the Orange Order is grounded in the collective memory and myths of wartime sacrifice, rather than the more mundane explanations of scholars such as Wilson (2007: 21):

> The Orange Order was more prevalent back in the fifties … it never really recovered from the war years, but in the fifties and early sixties it was still going. And I can remember seeing Orange lodges. Even after I first became an Orangeman, I used to go around the countryside—a little soldier—and find these old Orange halls—that's twenty something years ago. Today, you go by those same buildings that were there twenty-some-odd years ago, and they're gone, they're gone. You know, there just aren't any Orange halls, old Orange halls left. They've all closed down, they've been torn down, and the history is gone from that community … there's a small hamlet … and it's an antique store now. But originally, it was an Orange hall … had a great big King Billy up in the stained glass window … you know that little community was settled basically by Orangemen. They had a strong calling there. There hasn't been an Orange lodge there for fifty years.

For Pete, the Orange hall was a vibrant and going concern in the life of the community:

> The temple was just down the street, a few blocks, and it was a huge hall, it was gigantic … a three-floor apartment building now—but it was about … 750 seats easily, and we used to go there, and they used to have raffles and bingos and dinners. There was always something going on there. But I remember, even as a kid, most of the people were older, and as they passed away, keeping the building became harder and harder, and eventually they sold the building … my father lost interest, my father didn't have any interest, so that generation as a whole lost interest. My grandparents' generation had lots of interest. They were banging the drum and walking down the street you know and they would work hours and hours into it. We have stories of guys who bought their houses because the Orange hall was on the same street. That was the reason they bought that house.

Phil says: "I was born in 1949. My first Toronto parade is 1958, so we were in on the tail end of when the Order in Toronto was still measured in the thousands." Gavin situates himself in the longer history of the Canadian Orange Order:

> I was born in Orangeism because my father was an Orangeman ... Our Lodge was started back in the 1850s and ... the whole community belonged. As they grew old enough to join, they joined. I joined in 1951, when I was 20, 21 years old. It was the thing to do in the area. Everybody belonged to the Order, about every family, except the ones that were— that didn't want involvement with anything. Well, my father belonged and my brother joined just before he went in the services in'41. And then he passed on, so it's just myself.

With reference to the social history of rural Upper Canada (Ontario), Gavin notes that: "...when the people came from Ireland and Scotland, the first thing they built was church, the next one was the Orange hall. That was just the thing to do ... 'cos they were all Orange Protestants."

Many Orangemen speak with reverence about the rituals of induction, promotion, and continuity of the various "degrees" of the Orange Order. Given the fact that the Order has been losing membership for decades, and is now becoming precariously small in size and impact, the former days of glory, respect, and influence are recalled with nostalgia and some poignancy. A narrative of induction is recalled by George, who shed tears during his interview with us at his recollection of the passing of tradition from father to son:

> My father said "you want to come down to the Lodge tonight?" And I said "okay." He said "you better put on your school clothes," and we went down and walked into the hall. And those guys were maybe seventy years old, and they had beards, and all four or five of them were smoking pipes, you know? And then the old wood stove on, and the kettle was on top for to make tea later. And I was only 12 years old, and I walked in, and there was a block of wood that I guess was too big to move. So I sat in the corner there ... and the master, after five minutes or so, he said to my Dad, he said, "The boy going to join tonight?" And he was, you know, puffing away on his pipe, and my Dad just nodded his head ... maybe twenty minutes or so later the master said ... you'll have to go out and sit in the car for a while.... So then two big guys come out, oh they were over six feet, and they brought me to the under room and they said—asked me

a few questions, you know? They said like "are you a Protestant?" "Born to Protestant parents?" "You is young, but you're in charge of your own free will, and are you prepared to take an obligation to support Queen, country, and the Protestant cause?" So they said it's okay. So after I was initiated, the master said to me "now, he said, you've got one vote here, he said, the same as all the rest of us." And of course I was only twelve years old. I never said anything for probably two years, because all the guys were out there, were a lot older than me, you know? Like I say, there was maybe half a dozen of them with beards.

Another personal and affective account of the transmission of family heritage is presented by Jim:

When I was 20, before 1962, my grandfather was the strongest male figure in my life and in the home, and the Orange charter hung in our window along with the picture of the Queen's family, King and Queen, and Elizabeth as well. So I was quite familiar with what it was and I think perhaps I was more in tune with being a part of something my grandfather was a part of. And I learned why I was a member following that ... rather than ... political and aware world view of it, I was simply trying to be part of something that established me in a family atmosphere.

Jim continues: "Where some had a world view of it [the Orange Order], I more or less joined because of the emotional ties, and the family atmosphere."

A subset of the membership of the Canadian Orange Order are more recent immigrants from Northern Ireland or from Protestant roots in the UK. Art's contrastive narrative is typical of such a background:

There [in Northern Ireland] they tend to join more, sort of, if their parents are members, you know, if their fathers and mothers have been members, and they'll join. That's how I joined the lodge as a Junior. My dad was in the Lodge ... and I joined as a Junior and then it disbanded. But everyone was—I played soccer with a couple of guys in West Belfast, and they said "Do you want to join the Lodge?" I said okay. I started up again when I got to Manchester. And then I come over here and I didn't get back into it for maybe another ten years. But you gravitated towards people from Northern Ireland, okay, so there was obviously some sense of wanting to continue with your heritage and your roots ....

Bill, also from Northern Ireland, shares this concern to sustain: "the memory of the cultural traditions, the stories of the past, and so on ... you don't want this to die, you know, because over in Northern Ireland it's part of what you live with." Dave notes: "When I was at home [in Northern Ireland], you know it's from father to son, and grandfather... not so much here."

Here, we find a marked break with the experiences in Northern Ireland, where Orange identity is constructed and readily conveyed from generation to generation. Often, this occurs through the reproduction of collective memories and political myths used to develop strong senses of social categorization and long-term differences in cultural learning. In Northern Ireland, the passing on of the Orange tradition within the family, or other social networks within the community, is identifiable. Indeed, the notion of "family tradition" remains at the heart of membership. McAuley et al. (2011: 65) found that over 80% of members joined the Order through direct associations with family or friends. The *Orange Standard* (the equivalent of *The Sentinel*) in most editions can be found to display an array of photographs of family compositions involving several generations, those present ranging from young members of junior Lodges to those with long-service awards, for a quarter of a century, or longer, of continued membership. Such inter-generational experiences are almost entirely lost to the Order in Canada.

Among the membership is a strong shared sense of lamentation for the lost glories of the past Orange Order in Canada when it was a vital organization, operating on a grand scale, and elite in its connections to centers of power and authority. Lamenting how the Orange Order is currently misunderstood, Clive notes that "we used to come here [to the Orange hall] on Tuesday, and you couldn't get a seat." Pete offers a dramatic construction of the imagined influential past of the Canadian Orange Order in which Members of Parliament sat in Orange halls and received their voting mandate:

> ...okay, we're sitting in a room, "okay all the MPs, this is how we're going to vote," you know. And all the guys get together and say this is how we feel on this topic. Orangemen knew what the topics were—you know the big ones—you know, public schools, support for the military, you know, all these things were just common sense, you know. If you were an MP and an Orangeman, you were voted in by a bunch of Orangemen, and if

you voted against public schools, you weren't going to get a standing ovation at the next Lodge meeting, that's for damn sure. For damn sure, you weren't going to get a standing ovation.

Just as Pete acknowledges the diminished power and influence of the contemporary Canadian Orange Order, a matter of temporal change, like certain other participants, he is also alert to the spatial differences in settings between Canada and Northern Ireland, and thereby aware of the contrasting experiences and expectations of membership. While expressing appreciation for the mix of established Canadian and newly arrived members from Northern Ireland in the Canadian lodges, Pete explains how aspects of existence such as sectarian segregation, deep tribal loyalty, and inter-community violence are not present in the Canadian setting:

> ...you see, Canadians don't understand internal conflict. We don't have conflict. I mean, we have conflict like "we don't like Quebec," or something, you know. That's our conflict. But it's never really violent. You don't have to go to your car and look under your car and see if there's a bomb. You don't have to go and check your mirrors. There's guys [from Northern Ireland] who told us stories, you know, when they first moved to Canada, they didn't understand Canada.

While there is a generalized acknowledgment that the Orange Order is lacking the influence it once had in Canadian society, there is a defiance and a continued sense of hope and optimism that underpins narratives of membership and belonging in the contemporary era. Roy recounts the fraternal organizations that he and his father joined:

> ...what happened was my father was ill, and my father and I had joined the Masonic lodge together, we'd gone through all the degrees of the Masonic together, all the degrees of the Chapter together, all the degrees of the Preceptory together, all of the degrees of the Shrine together, so we had that. And you know he said to me, one day he said to me, you know, he said "the Shrine's okay, the Masons are okay, but doesn't compare to the Orange." And I said "Oh, come on, I'm tired of hearing this. They're a bunch of old men, and you know it's dying out, and it's this, and it's that, and it's the other thing." And he said "Well, you should investigate it before you make those statements."

Tom is among those participants who make the argument that the contemporary Orange Order is an attractive destination for those who are searching for their traditional roots:

I think we're entering a new age of search for meaning … I think the people are looking for foundation, roots, and there's so few places where you can expose yourself to people like yourself, ordinary people who have given some thought to why we're here, what do you want people to remember you by? …. And I think that Orangeism helps bring people to a forum where that can be explored…. I think we're actually going to see a resurgence because of the need to find some meaning in life.

Echoing these arguments and extending them into both an optimistic appraisal of the prognosis for growth and a strategy for recruitment and renewal of people searching for cultural meaning, family roots, and social anchoring, a blend of resignation, realism, and residual hope characterizes most contemporary Canadian Orangemen as they reflect on the future of the Orange Order. Jim's words are expressive of this perspective:

I tend to believe that where we [the Orange Order] are now, we're nearly at our lowest. I think we're at the point where we now need to, and will begin to, rebuild our membership. Our association will become more heritage based, people looking to find who they were in their family. But how we find members is irrelevant … and I do believe that it will bring about an increase in membership in time as we go along. Of course, society is changing drastically and becoming very criminally based and very violent in itself. I do believe the Orange Association provides a stability, a sense of stability and a family orientation that people would be looking for, that allows them to express themselves both in their faith and in their politics, very securely and very honestly, without reservation. I think there is a place for it 50 years from now…. What you need to do is find a new way to get it in the public eye that makes it more acceptable to them … the idea is to say what you have to say concisely, clearly, and in a modern way, that people will understand it. Because you're not, you're not trying to get members of your age in. You're trying to get members of a younger generation. And we also know our target membership is simply not going to be 18 year-olds, unless they come in with a father of 40, because 18 year-olds in society today are too busy trying to find themselves and their place in the world, and everything else.

Pete shares the perspective that: "you need to go out and engage people. That's what killed the lodges, a lot of them haven't engaged people." For Pete, the challenge is to engage people in preserving their heritage, but to do so in a way that is relevant to today.

At the core of contemporary Orange life in Canada is a compelling sense of brotherhood and fraternal affection. As Keith says: "Community is really the core of what happens here because this country is so large ... so community is really the key." On the basis of these bonds of friendship, the Orange Order continues as a congenial community and a center of conviviality. Illustrative of the warmth and affection of these bonds is the account that Mike offers of joining his church choir:

> When I came to Canada, I was aware of the fact that the Lodge was here, but I made no approach to it and joined the church ... and the children were baptized there and my oldest daughter, walked her down the aisle there, and so we had a long association with that church. And so I was conscripted into singing the bass section of the choir, and we were sitting there, and there was this big, comfy Irishman, also in the bass section, and he was speaking to a friend of mine who was sitting with the three of us in the bass section. And this time, I said to Keith, "well, how about joining the Lodge?" and Keith said "well, I don't know much about it," and so I looked around the corner and said "Well, I do." So Keith and I both joined.

George's memories of fraternal meetings are replete with accounts of conviviality and abundance. Describing the presence of one particular member, who was a Chief of Police in a local city, George recalls the evening with pride:

> ...like this guy is the chief of police ... and he's meeting on a Saturday night with 12 or 15 farmers. And after the thing would be over, you know there was all kinds of home cooked stuff. There's ... pies and stuff there, and the Lodge would always go over and buy a pound of cheese at the store, depending on how many people was there, and then, but everything else was all brought by the members. And I can remember ... they'd be telling stories ... and he [the police chief] would be laughing so that he'd take his glasses off, and the tears would be rolling down his eyes. And they'd leave—we'd leave—there probably 12 O'Clock on Saturday night after the Lodge. I mean, but I used to often wonder after, years after,

you know, what was the chief of police doing on Saturday night after the Lodge with about a dozen farmers, you know?

The relationship to alcohol is a matter of concern to a number of our participants, and they carry with them the cultural DNA of an organization that has struggled with the appropriateness of drinking since its inception in the early nineteenth century. To this day, certain lodges remain dry or abstemious, while others are open to alcohol. Speaking with some hyperbole, Roy says of a certain lodge:

> ...they've put out a brochure ... it talks about the social aspects of the Orange. We get together. We have a pint of beer. We play cards. We do this. That would never have happened when I came into the Orange. That—if that had happened, there would have been a Court Martial [sic].

Pete refers to one of the Toronto lodges that has "...a lot of abstainers, people who are in the Free Presbyterian Church and things like that." Ian says: "Our lodge is what they call an absentee [sic?] lodge, you know, so whenever anybody would be, you know, wanting to apply for membership ... we would tell them like there's no liquor or alcohol in the lodge, or at any functions ... now what a person wants to do in their own home, that's their own business."

The convivial and charitable aspects of Orange Order membership also emerge strongly from our discourse analysis of the Canadian Orange journal, *The Sentinel*. As can be seen in Fig. 6.1, we devised 15 categories based upon core Orange values and ideals. We then coded the entire content of each issue of *The Sentinel* (other than advertisements). Each time any of these categories appeared once or more often in a sentence, we counted it as one occurrence. Where a sentence contained more than one category, we counted it into two or more categories as appropriate. Altogether, there were 1859 mentions within the 15 categories across the 28 issues we coded. What is most striking is the relative absence of overt references to "faith, crown, and state" (McAuley and Tonge 2008). The term "Protestantism" (category 11—see Appendix A) occupies only 1.4% of all mentions, and there is an even less direct reference (0.6%) to the British connection (category 12). There are no references to the empire. The Crown and the monarchy (category 6) cover 7.3% of all mentions, and most of them are related to routine reportage of royal tours and encounters between prominent Orangemen and the royal

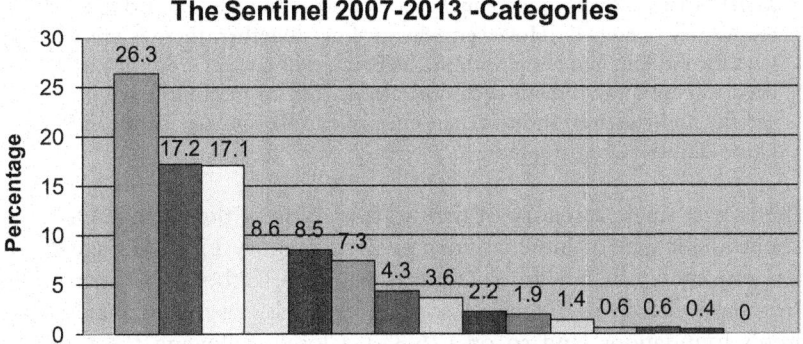
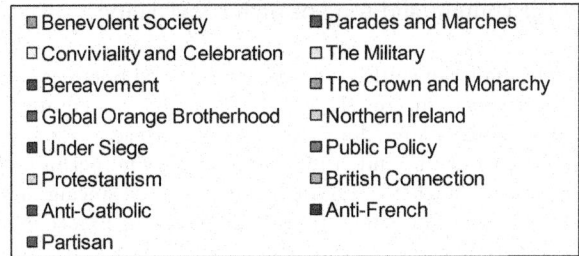

Fig. 6.1 The *Sentinel* 2007–2013—categories

family. Overtly, then, faith, crown, and state constitute less than 10% of all mentions. Having said this, while there are few specific mentions of Protestantism across the 15 categories, there is a distinguishable and pervasive Protestant theology, notably in the Chaplain's comments. In 2-2 (April 2004—p. 2), there is even a reference to "fanatical Protestant" as Grand Master Bill Johnston describes King Edward VI and his "intense persecution of Roman Catholics." When referring to the church, writers in *The Sentinel* tend to use Christian as a descriptor, rather than Protestant.

Of far greater prominence are categories that present the socially desired public face of contemporary Canadian Orangeism, combining moderation, patriotism, and proud charitable giving, with those categories that reference a fast fading and aging membership. The modal message might be paraphrased as follows:

> Many of us are dying, our branches are closing, and we find it difficult to recruit new members. However, when we get together, there is great fellowship and fun, and people admire us because of our generous giving. We need to constantly remind each other to get out to meetings, take part in parades and marches, and to retain our pride in the Orange Order and the old traditions [Our paraphrase].

The largest single category of mentions is those of the Orange Order as a benevolent society and charitable giving (category 1): to Orange charities, university scholarships (including one to a Catholic university), the Protestant churches, Alzheimer society, hospitals, juvenile diabetes, children's foundations, and so on (26.3%). Closely following the category of benevolent giving is that of conviviality and fellowship (category 3). Fully, 17.1% of all references are to having a good time. This report is typical of the content and tone of such conviviality:

> A delicious dinner of stuffed chicken with mashed potatoes and vegetables, followed by cherry cheese cake with tea or coffee was enjoyed while guests brought greetings. After dinner a dance took place with live music provided [by] Country Bound, a four piece band, who performed a selection of great music, much to everyone's enjoyment. Dancing and merriment went on into the late evening. (news from Harbour Breeze, Newfoundland in issue 136-2)

In issue number 2-4 from October 2004 (p. 11), there was a description of the visit of the Shankill Road Defenders to Brampton LOL #5. Describing them on the bus back from a day out in Niagara Falls, they: "…came back to the bus kitted out in Canada's colours with bright hats and Maple Leaf flags draped around their shoulders. Looked like they were on their way to celebrate July 1st never mind July 12th" (this was in the week of July 12).

The largest category that can be related to core Orange ideals is that of support for the military (category 4). The pages of *The Sentinel* are full of such references, and the various contributors routinely extol the bravery, duty, sacrifice, and loyalty of the military (8.6% of mentions): "the Loyal Orange Association has deep roots with our military, and we must let our Soldiers know that we stand behind them" (issue 136-3). Because they have become less frequent in recent years, Orange parades and marches, notably those in the marching season, are detailed with pride and encouragement (category 2). References to them include the messages that while they were small-scale, they were effective and showed off the Orange Order at its best, and they should be repeated in future years (17.2%): (a) "The Orange Association proved they are still alive in this fun regional parade [Niagara Grape and Wine Festival parade, 2007]" (issue 133-3); (b) "A parade is planned on June 6 2009, the first orange parade in Hamilton in over 30 years ... it is hope a large crowd will be in attendance to show Hamilton, and the world, what being an Orangeman is all about" (issue 135-1).

Perhaps unsurprisingly, the fifth single largest category of mentions is those of deaths and obituaries (category 5). A total of 158 deaths are reported across the 28 issues, and this makes up 8.5% of mentions. From 132-3 Summer 2006 (p. 23): "One unfortunate figure from the reports of the officers was the sad fact that deaths in the order substantially exceed the number of initiations." Other categories of note include mentions of Northern Ireland (category 8—3.6% of all mentions) and the global Orange brotherhood (category 7—4.3%). References to being under siege (category 9) are not overt, but there are a certain number of references to declining membership, branches closing, and the challenges of keeping Orangeism relevant today (2.2%): "Around our area we are having a few new members joining our ranks! I pray that this is the news we will be getting from other parts of the country as well!" (Grand Master Harry Thompson in issue 135-3)

Perhaps, the most rhetorical and declarative statement across the recent issues of *The Sentinel* is this one, which brings together the trauma of loss and decline with the defiance of persistent and proud spirit:

> ...lack of interest, decreased enrolments, competition from other groups, out migration, work commitments and death. He [Bro. Allen] told us that we cannot and must not, lose interest or surrender. We must work that much harder and face the challenges head on. We must strive for a better, brighter tomorrow! It is up to us to keep our standards high, for there can, must and will be a better tomorrow! "Brothers and Sisters we belong to a society that is built around some 214 years of history and pride. We will go forward and pass on what we have accomplished and WE WILL NOT SURRENDER [capitals in original], not today, not tomorrow nor in the future." (report of comments by Brother E. Allen at the Loyal Orange Association of Harbour Breton, December 28, 2009, in issue 136-2)

There are no anti-French (category 14) or anti-Catholic (category 13) sentiments in the pages of *The Sentinel*; however, there are a handful of references (less than 1%) to the problems of being *perceived* as anti-Catholic or anti-French. Issue 2-4 (October 2004—p. 9) has a reference to anti-French sentiments, but only to protest that the Orange Association is not in fact anti-French. There are no political party references (category 15) at all in the journal, and *The Sentinel* is definitely not the forum for the discussion and elaboration of public policy (category 10). Throughout the 28 issues, there are only a few mentions of public policy issues, and most of these are in passing or implicit. Pornography and crime rates are mentioned as social evils, and there is an implication that the current (Conservative) government is not doing enough to support the military. There is a feature in opposition to same-sex marriage legislation (issue 3-2; 16 mentions) and complaints about the absence of the Lord's Prayer in political institutions (133-1 and 134-2; 12 mentions in total) as well as objections to the habit of saying "happy holidays" instead of "happy Christmas" (133-1). There is also a small feature article on the death of Orangemen Thomas Scott at the hands of a nineteenth-century rebel, Louis Riel. Since Riel is now being recognized as a "father of Canadian confederation," the Orange Order believes it is important to remind Canadians that Scott was "murdered" by Riel and his men.

What concrete and definable benefits do our participants derive from membership in the Orange Order? What is in it for them? For some men, including Gavin, the Orange Order has provided an invaluable training in public speaking and organizational leadership. Jim points out: "... my complete vocabulary skill, and ability to converse with people, was learned from the Orange Lodge ...." For others, it was a needed social service. Phil points out that even as late as the 1970s, Orange Lodges with medical doctors were of value to ordinary members:

> I saw their membership list [a Lodge] from 1971. They had over 300 members, they had seven medical doctors ... why would they have seven medical doctors? Well, that's before national healthcare. You used to have to pay to go to the doctor. Again, it was the networking, and maybe if you were a brother and ... the doctor was in your Lodge, you might get in there for two dollars rather than three dollars.

While not generating a great deal of economic benefit today, there is a sense among the membership that the Orange Order was more influential in the days of large-scale and elite membership. Work obtained through family and community connections was of particular importance. Roy says:

> I can tell you that my father ... he did business like they do in the old country, you know. We bought from a butcher who was a Protestant, we had our hair cut by a barber who was a Protestant ... our electrician was a Protestant, and my father was very into that ... if he came to my house, he'd say "Who's the guy that's working on your plumbing?" and I say "I don't know. I just got him out of the yellow [pages]." "Ah," he says "he looks like an Italian to me"....

Trevor goes even further and says: "...the story goes at one time you couldn't get a job on the Toronto police service, the police force, unless you were an Orangeman. You couldn't even sweep the streets. I mean, that's how ingrained it was." However, in today's Orange Order, such advantages are negligible, and most of our participants disavow the practice.

For Pete, a critical facet of membership of the Orange Order is in supporting the membership and their families, and in respect, dignity, and caring for each other. Pete points out:

> I'm actually on the outreach committee. So, if you're sick and dying, I—well, until last year, I had two or three people I had to visit, and I visited once a month on behalf of the lodge. Those flowers there, exactly like those, those—what do they call them?—the paper flowers. Those go on the graves of old Orangemen, some that we've never even met, some that were from one hundred years ago. But we put those on the grave stones because when people go into that grave yard to see their family, they'll go "Wow, this guy, this guy got flowers. That stone's got to be one hundred years. Who could possibly be around to remember that guy?" And they'll go up to those flowers and we'll have a little tag on that says "Orange Lodge," and people will—you know, "these people take care of their own people."

How far is the current Orange Order open toward others in the broader Canadian community? To an extent, this brotherhood thrives on the security and comfort of being "among our own," and has designed a set of rituals to ensure that a sense of trust is developed within the organization, while a certain confidentiality is maintained toward the outside world. Indicative of certain aspects of the current mood may be a report of scholar David Wilson who interviewed a woman marching in the 2006 Toronto Orange parade. The woman's father had been a Canadian Grand Master. It materialized that her husband was a Catholic and had stayed home to look after the children. When Wilson asked her how her father had reacted to her marrying a Catholic, she gave a quintessentially Canadian and multicultural answer: "He was great ... he said 'As long as he loves you and makes you happy, I don't mind at all'" (Wilson 2007: 24). Our participant's accounts are full of narratives regarding cordial, even friendly relations with Roman Catholics. According to Dave, there is very little discussion of Catholics at lodge meetings.

The parallels with Northern Ireland are drawn by a number of participants, who contrast the sectarian and segmented character of Northern Ireland with the more liberal Canadian environment. Speaking of a fellow Canadian Orangeman returning from a trip to Northern Ireland, Gavin says: "…he'll come back from 12th of July and brag about how he walked down the street through the Catholic settlement, and proud of it, you know. Just antagonizing them, tormenting them …" Despite this rare instance of vicarious sectarianism, the majority of Orangemen do not adopt a negative view of Roman Catholics, and there is very little of the inter-religious conflict and discord that is witnessed in Northern Ireland.

While many of the Orangemen express a concern about the nature of new immigrants to Canada and their degree of loyalty to the traditions of Crown and country, none of them exhibit any overt racism. Clive's point of view, which we quoted in Chap. 3, is typical in this regard. Clive dismisses the accusation that the Orange Order is an "Irish KKK" as inaccurate and a slur. In fact, he argues, the Orange Order is both pluralistic and multiracial. Participants repeat that any person, no matter their race, would be admitted to membership. Mike reminds us that at the World Conference of the Orange Order, there are delegates from Ghana and Togo, and "… you don't have to be Irish, you don't have to be white, Anglo-Saxon protestant." Other participants make reference to

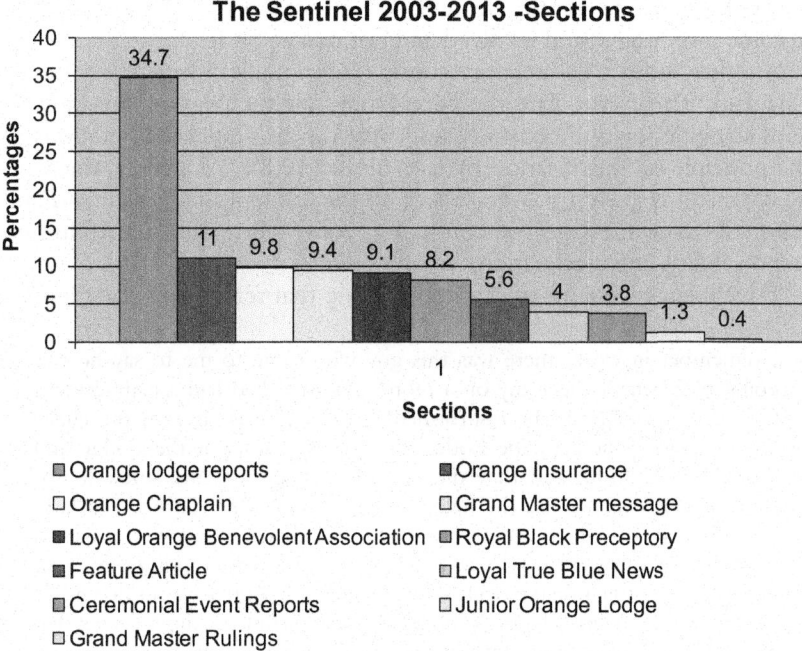

Fig. 6.2 The *Sentinel* 2003–2013—sections

the Italian Lodge, the Garibaldi Loyal Orange Lodge, and the leadership of Grand Master Dominic Di Stasi.

Respectability and recognition rank high among the status needs of Canadian Orangemen. Many of them in various ways exhibit a concern to be recognized for their good citizenship, their willingness to play by the rules, their loyalty, and their charitable giving. As Fig. 6.2 illustrates, the pages of *The Sentinel* focus on the community life of the Orange halls. The largest single section of *The Sentinel* consists of reports from various Orange Lodges and other societies around the country, which emphasize four core elements: celebration, conviviality, charitable giving, and rites of passage (34.7% of content). Very similar content is found in reports of the Royal Black Preceptory (8.2%). Spreadsheets and annual audits relating to the operations of Orange Insurance take up 11% of the content, while chatty messages from the Grand Master are a further 9.4% of content. A regular feature, the Grand Master's messages are pleasantly banal, but include gentle elements of exhortation for Orangemen to become more active and involved and not to lose pride.

Another substantial section consists of homilies from the Orange Chaplain. These articulate the core Protestant theology of the individual's struggle for righteousness, and they can be read as elaborations of the principle of "justification by faith alone" (9.8%). Together, the foregoing sections make up over 75% of all the content of *The Sentinel* and reflect its core messages of continuity, conviviality, outreach, fiduciary responsibility, and moderation.

Dave relates accounts of charitable giving that reflect Orange values:

> I remember in work, there was this guy who came to me to say he was going to a benefit for a guy on a motorcycle that had had a bad accident ... and his van had to be refurbished so he could use it with the chairlift ... came up here to the Lodge and told the story at the Lodge and they donated $500, and they didn't know the person, just knew it was somebody that could use the help to get this van done. Turned out later they discovered—which it didn't matter to us—that the guy was actually a Catholic. But it didn't matter to this Lodge ... there was another guy that was ... he was spina bifida, really badly challenged. And we went down, we did the same for him. Nobody bragged. We just did it. And I found that at the Orange Order you never pick up something [a gift or presentation cheque] that says "The Orange Order."

The Orangemen we interviewed have done their best to instill a sense of tradition and pride in their children. While this appears to have been moderately successful in certain respects, and it is clear that there is diffuse support for the Orange Order, it has proven very difficult to recruit a new generation to membership. As might be expected from the broader English Canadian context, if not according to certain stereotypes of Orangeism, there is a generalized liberalism and progressivism in the parenting styles of many of our participants. Harold says:

> ... if that's their choice, don't interfere. They're happy. And if they want to know something, we're here to answer. But don't push them into something that they don't want to do ... we never pushed our kids like—say you have to do this, you have to do this ... but if that's their choice, don't interfere. They're happy.

Referring to his son, Clive says: "… he walked in the 12th of July parades when he was a toddler you know [but] he just didn't have any interest in it. I didn't want to push it on him … If you pressure someone, you won't get a good member." Mike's 28-year-old son is a member, but his commitment has to be limited as he works two jobs and isn't always able to get to meetings. As Mike says: "He'd be an excellent member, and I try to encourage him to get him out more, but … I'm not paying his mortgage." Jim's children are also involved as members, but their levels of involvement are minimal. With reference to his son, Art says:

> My son was born there [Northern Ireland] too. We went on the parade. He was only a small little nipper. Just walked beside me and that's it. But I never kind of said to him over here [Canada] "do you want to join the Lodge?" I mean, he knows I'm in it. Couple of times he showed an interest, but then it's like—you know—soon as he shows an interest, it's [makes sound] *phtt*—you know, gone again, you know what I mean.

Unsurprisingly, recruitment from young men is very low, and this is the case even where there is a direct family involvement. For a range of reasons, cultural, economic, social, and political, membership no longer serves a purpose (Wilson 2007). Roy is strongly aware of the global reach of Orangeism and has undertaken a number of visits to international Orange conventions. His take on the future of the Orange Order is that declining religious observance is at the heart of declining numbers and that continued growth depends upon the sustaining of family loyalties. In our interview, Roy made reference to a marching band and showed us some yellowed photographs of Orange youth in uniforms from the 1970s. Despite fitful attempts to recruit new members, the band seems to be now long gone. In the end, Roy claims, the membership totals of the Orange Order, which have been in decline since the 1940s, have now "bottomed out" and are stabilizing, even growing somewhat. He refers optimistically to there being about 100 new members a year and so he claims: "1000 new members each decade—that's not too bad."

Other participants are less optimistic in their claims. The raw data are set out by Mike, who confirms that in 1965, there were 42 lodges in Toronto, but by 1972, this had diminished to 19 lodges. By 1992, there were only nine lodges remaining. Mike's own interest in the Orange Order started young, but it was not sustained:

> My first point of contact with the Orange order was when I was about six years old, and I tried to sneak into my father's barn to hear what they did when they held these meetings. And my brother and I laid up in the rafters of this barn for about half a day, and the rafters in our building were about this close. It's how they built farm buildings. Slate roofs, lights all hung below. You couldn't see if anybody was up there. We laid there for hours. Couldn't hear a damn thing.... And it must have been years later that my father said one day that he hoped that I'd enjoyed the meeting ... at that time, I had no interest. As I grew up and left school and was fourteen years old, and started riding motorcycles and became wild and crazy ....

A similar lack of adolescent interest in the Orange Order is evident in Keith's comments, when he says: "... forget about people until they're ... 25, 30 years old because they're too busy chasing skirts, getting married, courting, getting families started, getting careers started...." Phil raises a serious structural challenge to recruiting youth. Under the laws of the Orange Order, boys are required to be under the supervision of the Ladies' Orange Benevolent Association (L.O.B.A.), whose average membership is aging. Phil says: "... to be honest, if you look at the membership, I mean, the membership, the age of the L.O.B.A.—and they were the ones responsible for Juniors—I mean most of those ladies would be their grandmothers, if not their great grandmothers. So it's not something that they're going to do."

For Harold, Gavin, Jim, and Don, it is the attraction of newer organizations and meeting places, such as golf clubs, coffee clubs, and McDonalds, that now render the Orange halls less attractive. Don also mentions the challenges of getting his son (who "married a Catholic girl, but she wasn't strong Catholic") to either church or the Lodge. For Harold, it is the middle-aged generation that are the most suited to membership: "... as they get older and they get more mature, people get thinking more about it, and join later ... we find from 40 on ...." Roy agrees that it is the 40 year-olds who are at an ideal age for membership. As he says: "... by 40, you know what they're looking for ...." Don is among those participants who believe that the new rounds of membership to the Orange Order have skipped a generation, and that it is the grandsons, rather than the sons, who have an awakening interest as they mature.

How do contemporary Canadian Orangemen attempt to get the word out and to spread their ideas and share their perspectives on the world? As with many other organizations of this vintage, the Orange Order grew up relying upon the print media to spread the word. *The Sentinel* was for decades a daily newspaper of Orange opinion. Then, as membership and resources diminished, it became a weekly publication. In its most recent format, it has become an in-house magazine, published three or four times per year. On occasion, other forms of dissemination have been attempted, and it is clear that local Orange halls like to have their charitable giving recognized and acknowledged through the local media. As an organization with a declining membership and limited financial resources, it is challenging for the Orange Order to spread the word. Ironically, additional resources in the contemporary are become available as the Order closes halls and sells off real estate. As with other organizations that are in decline, they become richer in cash assets as they diminish in membership.

Jim and Harold are two members who regard *The Sentinel* as largely irrelevant to the development of Canadian Orangeism. Jim points out both that they receive more information from Northern Ireland than they do from Canadian sources, and that the Canadian Orange leadership has not been successful in keeping its own membership informed. Harold is disappointed with *The Sentinel*, both for the growing infrequency of its distribution and for its predominant style as a "social club" rather than a journal of advocacy.

When it comes to telling the Orange story, the July 12 parades retain a great deal of importance on the membership. The participants are uniform in expressing pride and joy in the planning, preparations, and execution of the parades, and they regard them as a continued channel for the undiluted manifestation of Orangeism to the broader Canadian community. "Who does not love a parade?" is the common rhetorical question. Answering that question sincerely raises the question as to the ongoing relevance and practicality of the street parade as a manifestation of Orange values and the Orange tradition.

Clearly, the annual parade retains a deep emotional significance as a source of community pride for men such as Harold, Jim, and Dave, who can recall marching in parades from a young age. Dave says: "... we went down to see the Orange parade in Toronto and it was massive then [in 1962]. It was a big parade then." With reference to tiger lilies, Harold says "... there was orange lilies and they always grew wild and ... you'd put them on the hood of your car and you'd go in the parade." As Jim reminisces of his years in the flute band:

> There wasn't one person that didn't go to the 12th of July parade ... the whole country stopped ... Up and down the side streets all around and through the whole neighbourhood practicing for the 12th ... really a time of excitement for me, and anticipation. And of course on that day of the 12th, my grandfather would get dressed up, he would have his bath two hours early ... get dressed with his best clothes on, and his ribbons and sash, and he'd head off to the street car.

For Mike, the key point of contact with the parade was in practicing for the marching band: "I was a member playing with the ... flute band at the time. We played annually for that lodge and ... some of the band members were lodge members, and others used to attend our practice.... My Grandfather was co-founder of the flute band just after World War One." The parade is an opportunity to manifest and promote Orange traditions and values in a public way. Pete raises the public policy issue of the presence of Orangeism in the public sphere:

> The gay flag flies from City Hall, and the Acadian, which is the French flag, flies there and they put it on for whatever group or event, right? The Caribbean I think flies there. Different ones. So we said, you know, the 12th of July we want our flag put up there, and that's one of our issues....

In contrast with Northern Ireland, according to Roy, the Canadian parades tend to be much more relaxed and low-key. He says: "It's always held in the evening, and it's a different style of march. It's not a military style, like back home [in Northern Ireland], it's a sauntering. They sort of just saunter along and they talk to their neighbours ... 'Oh hey, Bill! How are you? How's your wife?' You know? ... It's more like a stroll." And yet, there is a sad sense of resignation among some participants at the ultimate futility of the parades. Clive questions the decision to allocate large amounts of money to produce leaflets to hand out at the parade when: "...there's nobody looking at you really. You know, they walk through the ranks on you ... so what are you doing here? They don't hear you." Dave laments the lack of attention and press coverage devoted to the Toronto parade each year, and Art notes even of would-be supporters: "Guys can't be bothered with it anymore. They're standing in the pub when the band goes by." Harold sums up the sense of futility in this reflection on what ordinary Canadian bystanders think when they see the Orange parade go by:

> They haven't got a clue ... They ask "what is this?" You know? "What is this about?" ... but yet if they have a Gay parade in Toronto ... they knows what it is. You see, the media is pretty well against us, you see? ... They don't give us any coverage, and any coverage they do give us—a lot of untruths.

This perspective is shared by Tom, Trevor, and Pete. Pete points out that while there is a generalized ignorance, it is usually benign.

What remains for most participants, despite the lamentation regarding getting the message across, is a residual sense of hope. It would be challenging to carry on as an organization without some sense that the future might see a turnaround. If the journal is of decreasing relevance and the current budget for leafletting ineffective, and if the Orange parades do not have the impact that they once did, then where is the sense of hope? For Mike and Pete, it rests in the promise of new technology, notably social media. Referring to the waves of applications for information regarding the Orange Order that followed the introduction of the Orange website, Mike says:

> ...when we first put our website forward ... there was a place where you could apply for information ... so we're looking at new ways to be creative and get people interested in it again ... a result of electronic enquiry ... and people liked what they saw. You see, the problem is they largely don't know what they're getting into until once they've joined it, you know?

The notion of community is deeply ingrained and meaningful for today's Canadian Orangemen. Answers to questions surroundings their heritage, where have they come from, their traditions, and values remain core to membership and in most cases are readily answered. Much less easily responded to are other questions involving the understanding of community, how it is to be sustained, and solidarity involving the inter-generational transmission of core tenets and beliefs. To be sustainable as a community, the values and attitudes need to be passed on, and younger members, whether family or not, need to be recruited to replace and sustain the membership. Part of this passing on will involve an understanding of collective memory and learning how to tell their story. At the moment, this seems barely viable. It is something that almost all the Orange community are aware of, but are unsure of how to come to terms with.

REFERENCES

Kaufmann, Eric. "The Orange Order in Ontario, Newfoundland, Scotland and Northern Ireland: A Macro-social Analysis." In *The Orange Order in Canada*, edited by D.A. Wilson, 42–68. Four Courts Press: Dublin, 2007.

McAuley, James W. *Very British Rebels? The Culture and Politics of Ulster Loyalism*. New York: Bloomsbury, 2016.

McAuley, James W. & Jon Tonge. ""Faith, Crown and State": Contemporary Discourses within the Orange Order in Northern Ireland." *Peace and Conflict Studies* 15.1. (2008): 136–155.

McAuley, James W., Jon Tonge, & Andrew Mycock. *Loyal to the Core? Contemporary Orangeism and Politics in Northern Ireland*. Dublin: Irish Academic Press, 2011.

Wilson, D.A. "Introduction." In *The Orange Order in Canada*, edited by D.A. Wilson, 9–24. Four Courts Press: Dublin, 2007.

CHAPTER 7

Conclusion

Abstract In this brief chapter, McAuley and Nesbitt-Larking offer a summary of the principal findings throughout the book, on the contemporary Canadian Orange Order and perspectives on Faith, Crown, State, and Community. The authors return to the theoretical perspectives of Social Identity/Self-categorization theory, the politics of commemoration, and English Canadian exceptionalism, in order to assess the findings as a whole. A brief discussion of limitations of the study and a prospectus for future work concludes the chapter.

Keywords Orange Order · Faith · Crown · State · Community

Given what we can discern of the contemporary Orange Order and Orangeism in Canada, we would be hard pressed to concur with McAuley and Tonge's assessment of the situation in Northern Ireland. For many Protestants in Northern Ireland, the Orange Order "continues to offer a central focus for social life and … retains an important cultural and religious influence in many parts of Northern Ireland" (McAuley and Tonge 2008: 137). However, what remains of the Canadian Orange Order in the dwindling number of Orangemen constitutes a valuable living archive of an eighteenth- and nineteenth-century social order of crown, faith, and the imperial state. Throughout this book, we have attempted to open up this archive as a living archaeology and anthropology of those who find themselves increasingly "out of time" in both senses of that expression.

From our content and discourse analysis, it is apparent that the public face of the Orange Order remains focussed on the preservation of a highly generalized Protestantism and a continued loyalty toward the Crown and associated symbols of the British connection, notably the Canadian military. Our interview participants are Protestant, but more generically Christian, and not particularly observant. There is a diffuse and sentimental attachment to the monarchy, but little overt interest beyond the standard rituals of loyalty to the Crown. Characterizing Orangemen today as in their Canadian past is a powerful liberal individualistic belief in freedom that owing to North American history has gradually become detached from the British connection, traditional conservative values, and the monarchy. This has resulted in a complex set of values regarding faith, crown, and state. They are, in the main, not anti-Catholic, or sectarian, in any meaningful sense of the word, and are anti-Quebec separatism rather than anti-French per se. There is little of the imperial connection to Britain, and a rather remote interest in the affairs of Northern Ireland among many of them, the connection being made in terms of Protestantism rather than in any deeper political sense. There is, however, a staunch support and loyalty to the Canadian Crown, notably its armed forces and military traditions.

The words of our participants and the pages of *The Sentinel* also show that while there are some sentimental bonds of historical connection with Northern Ireland and the broader Orange community, there is little overt mention of Protestantism or the British heritage of Canada, and there is no partisanship, anti-Catholicism or overt anti-French sentiment. What dominates the pages of *The Sentinel*, as well as the comments of our interviewees, is a genial conviviality in which the celebration of community through food, music, and togetherness is combined with the charitable giving of the Orange Order as a benevolent society. Counterpoised against this life-affirming celebration are the multiple notices of death that are further implicit in the ever-shrinking coffers of Orange Insurance with its emphasis on life insurance policies.

We will conclude with some reflections on the three theoretical traditions that we have used throughout our analyses: Social Identity Theory/Self-categorization Theory; the distinctiveness of English Canadian political culture; and memory and the construction of identity. What we have discovered is that even the most robust and ideologically coherent traditions and values will adapt to their historical conditions and their social settings. Our account of the contemporary Orange Order in Canada is illustrative in detail of how this takes place.

A core understanding of Social Identity Theory and Self-categorization Theory is that identities are flexible, malleable, and adaptive, and that they develop in response to the social relations in which they are situated. Identities are verbs rather than nouns, and they emerge strategically and tactically in a field of social forces. Certain settings prefer and privilege a range of possible categorizations, identifications, and comparisons, and these are framed by those entrepreneurs of identity who are best able to command attention and define reality. In such contexts, for instance in Northern Ireland, a clear and consistent line on social identity and social inclusion and exclusion is maintained.

In an environment, such as contemporary English Canada, in which the structural bases of sectarianism are largely absent, and in which communities and families are mixed, those that attempt to define and delimit Orangeism in a rigid and doctrinaire manner are largely unsuccessful. Their relatively extreme views may be tolerated within the larger group, but explained away as anachronistic, somewhat embarrassing, or better related to conditions and circumstances in Northern Ireland. Our interviews are full of contrastive comments between the Orange Order of the past and the contemporary movement, as well as contrastive comments regarding sectarian divisions and conflict in Northern Ireland, and the state of play in Canada.

Canadian Orangemen express their loyalty toward their British heritage, the monarchy, and the Protestant faith in the terms of their evolving identities. While proud of their British origins and family connections, many of the participants are Canadians first, give priority to the Canadian Anthem over the Royal Anthem, celebrate the Canadian Armed Forces, and consider themselves subjects of the Queen of Canada. They are loyal to the Crown, but also appreciate the context in which the monarchy is in question and monarchical forms of government are considered irrelevant and obsolete. Many Orangemen have developed a postmodern approach toward the monarchy, grounded in contingency and a transactional approach toward the persons who occupy the various roles. This reflects acceptance of a disenchanted and personalized view of the monarchy that is distinct from the compliance of traditional authority. For most Orangemen, loyalty is expressed toward the Canadian Crown rather than the British Crown.

Canadian Orangemen define themselves as Protestants in broad spirit if not always in observance and practice. Their religious observance accentuates the personal and voluntaristic aspects of Protestant theology. Such an identity is compatible with a generalized self-identification as "Christian" and with a broad acceptance of Roman Catholics as neighbors and even friends or family members.

Perhaps, the most revealing set of responses among the participants relates to their identifications regarding homosexuality and gay rights. Operating from a social conservative ideological basis, Canadian Orangemen navigate the question of gay rights and homosexual equality in a range of ways. At the extremes, there are those few who continue to regard homosexuality as an abomination and oppose rights for gay people, and those who have welcomed gay people into their lives and would have no objection to gay men joining the Orange Order. For the most part, the perspective of Canadian Orangemen is that of "don't ask, don't tell." This is a limited tolerance for homosexuality, and a brittle, restricted acceptance that requires gay men to make no demands and expects them not "flaunt" their sexuality. In line with the perspective of social conservatives on a range of issues, many participants repeat the phrase: "equal rights for all; special rights for none."

The historical setting for Canadian Orangemen is that of evolving English Canadian political culture. What has become of Orangeism in Canada over the past 200 years belies the readily available stereotypes of the Orange Order and resists oversimplification. Orangemen have not only been prompted to adapt through the exigencies of political and social life in Canada but have also creatively elected to do so under certain circumstances. It is clear that among the most powerful irritants for Canadian Orangemen today are those mediated and popular views of the Order as racist, discriminatory, hostile toward Others, reactionary, and secretive. Our participants counter such views at every opportunity.

The complexity of Orange identities in the Canadian context has been well explored by historians such as Kaufmann who explains the origins of pragmatism and moderation among the Orange leadership of the nineteenth century, notably in the ideas of Ogle Gowan and the accommodations reached between Macdonald and Cartier. The "Orange-Green-Bleu" post-1836 alliance united Irish and French Catholics with Ontario Orange Protestants against the rebels and those who would seek to supplant the British connection (Kaufmann 2007: 64). As we point out in Chap. 2, in the context of elite accommodation and the political balances of nineteenth-century Canada, an unvarnished Protestant loyalism, along with demands for rigid uniformity, unilingualism, monologism, and monoculturalism, could not survive. As Greg Kealey has written, while Crown, empire, and the Protestant faith remained abiding and powerful principles, they had to be reworked in the context of the Canadian polity (Kealey 1995).

Above all else, in the context of post-war Canada of the past 70 years, Wilson (2007) identifies dominant sociocultural and political changes that have called into question the very bases of the Orange Order. First, the decline of the British connection and the rise of a civic English Canadian nationalism; second, the growth of a complex and ethnically diverse society beyond the "two nations" of the English and the French; third, an increasingly secular society in which religiosity and church attendance have been in decline; and, finally, the rise of a Welfare State that has undercut the need for the mutual societies of the nineteenth century. Not only have these changing circumstances conditioned a decline in Orange membership but they have also conditioned and opened up modes of adaptation among contemporary Orangemen. This is why many of our participants understand and generally support the broad principles of an inclusive Canadian multiculturalism, a value which is strongly embedded in English Canadian society. Participants further refer to the Charter of Rights and Freedoms as a foundational document of the Canadian polity, and they self-define as more open, tolerant, and liberal than their counterparts in Northern Ireland.

In the context of a secular Canadian society, where there are few markers of overt sectarianism, or the binding of a Protestant identity to forms of national purpose, there is both encouragement and space for more cordial social relationships between Protestants and Catholics, as well as with other groups and communities. Our research participants exhibit strong support for religious tolerance, dialogue, and mutual respect among religious communities. They reflect the views of the former Grand Master who, according to Wilson, told his daughter who had married a Roman Catholic: "As long as he loves you and makes you happy, I don't mind at all" (Wilson 2007: 24).

However, the core ideological orientation remains socially conservative, even if few pay more than limited support, at the ballot box, to Canada's Conservative Party. There is widespread and largely uncritical support for the Canadian military and "our men in uniform."

Moreover, there is a widespread suspicion of "political correctness" and perspectives that call into question the core righteousness of the White Anglo-Saxon Protestant (WASP) identity. Their social conservatism emerges most evidently in attitudes toward Muslims and Islam, and anti-Muslim sentiments are evident in some of the interviews we conducted. Opposition toward Muslim immigrants is grounded both in the realistic conflict of concern regarding the distribution of societal resources and access to public goods, and perceptions of symbolic threat over the question of core Canadian values.

The multiculturalism that Canadian Orangemen support is one that is identified with long-standing conservative communitarianism that is identified with the Crown, and is opposed to the "deux nations" approach of Quebec nationalism. Among the participants, there is a widespread and uniform hard line when it comes to swearing allegiance to the Queen, and a perspective that those who do not wish to do so can "go home."

Where support for progressivism and a more generalized liberalism becomes apparent is in the attitudes of the participants toward parenting. When it comes to the transmission of Orange values from one generation to the next, the Orange Order has clearly suffered from a lack of recruitment and the relative failure of intergenerational transmission. The perspectives of most Orangemen are voluntaristic and liberal. With regard to their children, they say "it's their choice," "leave them alone," and "don't push." Many believe that attempting to recruit young men is a lost cause and that the pool of potential recruits is more middle-aged, those who have established careers and have older children. It is difficult to replicate the familial and community bonds that exist in Northern Ireland. As Bill puts it: "Over in Northern Ireland, it's part of what you live with." Our participants know their traditions well and are proud of their roots. They share a cohesive community, but their orientations toward the broader Canadian community are mixed.

They are frustrated that few revere the past, appreciate the sacrifices that have been made, and affirm the glories of British North America of the past. There is an insistence on the part of the Orangemen that new Canadians should understand the principles of constitutional monarchy that bind Canada to its past and, for them, undergird its future. They revel in past glories, including the defeat of American republicanism in the War of 1812, the triumph of the British military in overcoming the rebellions of 1837, the execution of Louis Riel in 1885, and the Battle of Vimy Ridge in 1917. There is a deep sense of collective memory, an understanding of the past, which helps individuals locate themselves in and make sense of the present. As such, collective memory is at the core of the contemporary Orange community. Knowledge and narratives about a particular past, and particular ways of viewing it, are crucial in identity construction.

There is some limited hope and optimism for a revivification of the Canadian Orange Order, but it is mixed with much nostalgia and lamentation at the lost glories of the past. Not only is there an emphasis on the bravery, loyalty, duty, and sacrifice of previous generations of Orangemen, but there is also a pride in the historical relevance and prominence of the Order. Here, the organization has a problem in terms of whether people are actively engaging with the Orange narrative and, if so, who is listening to the narrative produced. But these Orange Order cultural traditions have not been reinforced through any widespread generational transmission of values or communal solidarity.

As a result, the Order's monarchical and pro-British stance seems dated, especially when an increasingly heterogeneous immigration policy has led to the development of a more multicultural civic culture. As Canadian political culture has modernized, religion has become less influential. The development of the Canadian welfare state has also undermined the Order's role as a provider of sickness and death benefits to members. Thus, the values of an organization founded in eighteenth-century Ireland have become decreasingly relevant in twenty-first-century Canada.

Perhaps, we may leave the last words with Jim and his assessment of what being a member for long years means to him:

> …the idea is that we have the opportunity to make sure that our children grow in this society understanding that we are all different and we all have different opinions, faith and cultural heritage … this is the idea, no one should be greater than the other one … but should be equally recognized. In this perfect world that we—Orangeism—hoped that we were building as we were coming along, through Canada and civil services, and everything else, and political, the perfect world, and in many cases our rights to support freedom of speech and of religion has put us on the back burner, because of everyone else being able to take advantage of it. Our numbers have so diminished we didn't keep up with that, and now, what we had hoped to create is our own demise because here we are, everyone else has

benefited from what we, politically, promoted through all different societies, and here we are now ... our voice is so much diminished and we are so much smaller than we were. But I do believe that multiculturalism is an asset and it should be within our association as well ... and our children know more about Canada and Toronto and in particular being multicultural, than you and I will ever know.

Whether the Order can continue to adapt to meet Jim's vision, what form it shall take, and indeed whether there is an Orange Order in the future are questions for further consideration. To survive and even to thrive, Orangemen need to rediscover a sense of leadership, purpose, and direction, characteristics which seem to be lacking in the contemporary phase. The Order was originally seen as a specifically immigrant and ethnic institution, working to further a particular community within the population. It has altered much, sometimes reluctantly in the light of changed social, economic, and political conditions. In the end, what is left of the Orange Order is a small group of loyal and devoted men, who take pride in their charitable work, their community spirit, the values that they uphold, and the community bonds that they share. They take solace in their own sense of moral decency and righteousness, and they share a comfortable sense of belonging, of being at home in a convivial and worthy brotherhood.

References

McAuley, James W. & Jon Tonge. ""Faith, Crown and State": Contemporary Discourses within the Orange Order in Northern Ireland." *Peace and Conflict Studies* 15.1. (2008): 136–155.

Kaufmann, Eric. "The Orange Order in Ontario, Newfoundland, Scotland and Northern Ireland: A Macro-social Analysis." In *The Orange Order in Canada*, edited by D.A. Wilson, 42–68. Four Courts Press: Dublin, 2007.

Kealey, Gregory. "Orangemen and the Corporation: The Politics of Class in Toronto During the Union of the Canadas." In *Workers and Canadian History*, edited by Gregory Kealey, 163–208. Kingston: McGill-Queen's University Press, 1995.

Wilson, D.A. "Introduction." In *The Orange Order in Canada*, edited by D.A. Wilson, 9–24. Four Courts Press: Dublin, 2007.

Appendix A

Categories for Discourse Analysis

1. References to charitable works and benevolent society functions.
2. References to parades, marching, and marching season.
3. References to conviviality and celebration.
4. Support for the military and troops.
5. Bereavement, death announcement, and obituary.
6. Loyalty to the Crown and monarchy.
7. References to the global Orange brotherhood.
8. References to Northern Ireland or unionism.
9. Siege mentality.
10. Statements on other public policy issues—immigration, gun control, social conservative issues on family, and sexuality.
11. Defense of Protestantism.
12. Loyalty to the British connection/empire.
13. Anti-Catholicism.
14. Anti-French sentiment.
15. Partisan political references—notably conservatism.

Appendix B

Names (Pseudonyms) and Data on Participants

Names	Age	Educ	Political party
Art	52	High	Abstain
Bill	47	High	Conservative
Chris	67	High	Abstain
Clive	68	High	Conservative
Dave	74	High	New Democratic Party
Don	82	High	Conservative
Gavin	81	University	Conservative
George	70	High	Conservative
Harold	77	Some high	Conservative
Ian	74	Some high	Abstain
Keith	70	High + dip	Conservative
Mike	66	High	Conservative
Pete	28	University	Conservative
Jim	59	Some High	Conservative
Phil	64	Some Univ	Conservative
Roy	82	University	Conservative
Tom	72	University	Conservative
Trevor	63	College	Unknown
N =	18		
Mean =	66.444		
Std Dev =	13.544		

Appendix C
The Orange Order and Orangeism in Canada

Interview Prompts

1. What was your first point of contact with the Orange Order?
2. What made you decide to join the Orange Order?
3. Do other family members belong to the Orange Order? Who are they?
4. Do you attend church? How often?
5. Do you consider yourself a devout Protestant?
6. What is the role of Protestantism in Canada today?
7. Does your faith influence your political views in any way?
8. Should children be required to recite the Lord's Prayer in public schools today?
9. Are you a monarchist?
10. Do you consider Canadians to be loyal enough to the Queen?
11. Is the monarchy in Canada under threat today? If so, from what or whom?
12. New Canadians currently swear allegiance to the Queen. Do you agree that this requirement should be dropped?
13. Should children be required to sing God Save the Queen in school on ceremonial occasions?
14. Have you ever marched with the Orange Order in public? When and where?
15. Do you still march with the Orange Order? If so, why? If not, why not?

16. What impression do you believe Canadians get when they see Orange marches?
17. What differences do you think there are between the Orange Order in Canada and the Orange Order in the old country? (if probed, Northern Ireland and Scotland).
18. Do you follow events in Northern Ireland? How interested are you in what is going on in Northern Ireland?
19. Which of the following benefits do you believe that you receive from belonging to the Orange Order? (a) social/friendship; (b) cultural heritage; (c) religious; (d) political connections and information; (e) economic advantages; (f) family bonds; and (g) insurance against needs.
20. How relevant is the Orange Order in contemporary Canadian society?
21. How far do you believe young Canadian descendants of Protestant heritage are keeping the faith? Do they go to church? Do they remain loyal to the Queen? Are they joining Orange Lodges?
22. Do you believe that Quebeckers are loyal to Canada or not loyal enough?
23. Should Quebeckers be considered one of the two founding nations of Canada or one of ten equal provinces?
24. Should French be an official language of Canada?
25. Much is made these days of homosexual rights in Canada. Do you believe that homosexuals have too few rights, too many rights, or about the right amount?
26. Aboriginal Canadians often refer to the Royal Proclamation of 1763 and claim to be loyal to the Queen. How far do you believe this to be the case?
27. Canada is often said to be a multicultural society. How far do you believe that multiculturalism and Orangeism are compatible?
28. In general terms, what kind of future is there for the Orange Order in Canada?
29. Should new Canadians conform to our values?
30. If a federal election were to be held today, who would you vote for? (if probed, which way might you lean?)
31. As you know, we all have role models and those we look up to. Thinking of Canadians, past and present, who do you regard as your heroes? You may name one or two people.

32. What is your age?
33. What is or was your primary occupation?
34. What was the highest level of education you attained?

INDEX

A
Anglican, 25, 37

B
Bilingualism (official), 74
Boer War, 1899–1902, 75
British and Commonwealth Succession to the Crown Act, 2013, 52
British North America, 14, 15, 26, 51, 65, 114

C
Catholicism, 7, 15–18, 20, 26–28, 37, 39, 64, 73, 110, 117
Catholic, (Roman), 6, 22, 27, 28, 33–37, 39, 40, 79, 100, 112
Celebration, 17, 29, 50, 101, 110, 117
Charitable giving, 95, 96, 101, 102, 105, 110
Charity, 96
Chosen glories, 8, 47, 50

Chosen traumas, 8, 47, 50, 80, 82
Christian/Christianity, 22, 23, 27, 32, 40–44, 50, 53, 69, 95, 110, 112
Clarke, Edward Frederick, 18
Congregationalist (s), 29
Conservative Party, 5, 7, 18, 19, 50, 70, 113
Constitution Act (British North America Act), 1867, 51
Conviviality, 17, 93, 96, 101, 102, 110, 117
Crown, 5–7, 14, 15, 20, 42, 45, 47, 48, 52–57, 60, 68, 69, 75, 94, 95, 109–111, 114, 117

D
Dennison, William, 67, 68
Derry, Siege of, 64
Diefenbaker, John, 3, 49, 67
Disraeli, Benjamin, 18
Di Stasi, Dominic, 101
Durham, Lord, 15

© The Editor(s) (if applicable) and The Author(s) 2018
J.W. McAuley and P. Nesbitt-Larking, *Contemporary Orangeism in Canada*, DOI 10.1007/978-3-319-61842-5

E
Emigration, 26, 64
Evangelism, 27

F
Fenian Raids, 1866, 75
Ferguson, George, 67
Ferguson, G. Howard, 18, 67
First World War, 1914–1918, 48, 76
French Canada, 18, 53, 64, 73, 74
Frost, Leslie, 21, 67

G
Gowan, Ogle, 16, 19, 112
Grand Lodge of British America, 16
Grand Orange Lodge of Canada, 65

H
Harper, Stephen, 49–51
Henry, George, 67
Hinduism, 27
Homosexuality, (Gay Rights), 71, 72, 112
Hume, David, 6
Huron University College, 8

I
Immigration, 7, 14, 23, 50, 53, 55, 58, 115, 117
Indigenous peoples, 53, 55, 56
Ireland, 16, 19, 21, 25–27, 36, 48, 65, 66, 77, 80, 88, 115
Islam, 7, 27, 42, 43, 114
Islamophobia, 45

K
Kennedy, Thomas, 67
Knights of Columbus, 39, 41

L
Ladies' Orange Benevolent Association (L.O.B.A.), 104
Laurier, Sir Wilfrid, 55
Leinster, 25
Liberalism, 8, 69, 102, 114
Liberal party, 5, 14, 18, 19, 23, 113

M
Macdonald, Sir John A., 3, 18, 19, 51, 55, 112
Manitoba Schools Question, 1890, 75
McAuley, James W., 2, 5, 8, 25, 50, 65, 66, 85, 90, 94, 109
McGee, Thomas D'Arcy, 16
Memory, 8, 47, 64, 76, 82, 87, 90, 108, 110, 115
Methodist (s), 25, 29
Migration, 25, 27, 63, 97
Monarch (ism) (ist), 58, 69, 70, 72, 121
Monarchist League, 37
Monarchy, 7, 45, 48–60, 67, 69, 73, 80, 94, 110, 111, 114, 117, 121
Multicultural, 8, 23, 50, 53, 54, 100, 115, 116, 122
Multiculturalism, 8, 49, 50, 53, 55, 58, 68, 113, 114, 116, 122
Muslim, 23, 42, 43, 45, 114

N
National anthem (of Canada), 44, 57, 69
Nesbitt-Larking, Paul W., 2, 8, 49
New Brunswick, 16, 22
Newfoundland, 16, 18, 21, 22, 75, 96
Northern Ireland, 2, 6, 8, 9, 27, 32, 36–40, 45, 56, 69, 71, 77–80, 89–91, 97, 100, 103, 105, 106, 109–111, 113, 114, 117, 122
Northern Irish, 4, 6, 80

O

Ontario, 3–5, 8, 15, 16, 18, 19, 21, 22, 26, 64, 66, 67, 82, 86, 88, 112
Orangeism, 1–3, 6, 8–10, 15, 16, 19–23, 25–27, 32, 41, 47, 52, 53, 58, 63–68, 73, 76, 77, 80–82, 88, 92, 95, 97, 102, 103, 105, 106, 109, 111, 112, 115, 122
Orangeman, 2–10, 13, 16–23, 27–29, 31, 33–45, 47, 48, 50, 51, 53–58, 60, 65–70, 72–76, 80–82, 86–88, 90, 92, 94, 97–102, 105, 107, 109–116
Orange Mutual Benefit Fund, 18
Orange Order, 2–6, 8–10, 13–22, 26–30, 32, 34, 38–41, 44, 48, 50, 52, 55, 63–66, 68, 70–72, 76, 78–82, 86–94, 96–100, 102–105, 107, 109–116, 121, 122
Orange Standard, 9, 90
Orange, William of, 47
Oronhyatekha, Dr., 55

P

Parade (s), (Orange), 2, 3, 5–9, 15, 16, 20, 22, 23, 27–38, 40–45, 48–60, 65–79, 81, 82, 86–107, 109, 110, 113–116, 121
Perth Agreement, 52
Presbyterian (s), 25, 29, 30, 94
Protestant (ism), 3, 5, 15–17, 19, 26–29, 31, 32, 37, 43–45, 47, 52, 55, 65, 68, 72, 99, 113, 114, 122

Q

Quebec, 15, 16, 19, 50, 52, 53, 64, 66, 67, 73, 74, 91, 110, 114

R

Rebellions of 1837, 114
Riel, Louis, 16, 82, 98, 114
Royal Anthem, 51, 56, 57, 111
Royal Proclamation, 1763, 55, 122

S

Salvation Army, 28
Scott, Thomas, 16, 82, 98
Second World War, 1939–1945, 21, 56, 76
Sectarian, 6, 32, 38, 91, 100, 110, 111
Sectarianism, 39, 40, 45, 100, 111, 113
Secularism, 41
Self-categorization Theory, 7, 110
Sentinel, 2, 5, 9, 18, 19, 21, 48, 90, 94–98, 101, 102, 105, 110
Sikhism, 27
Social Identity Theory, 7, 110

T

Toronto, 3, 5, 6, 8, 14, 17, 18, 20, 21, 23, 34, 53, 66–68, 88, 94, 99, 100, 104, 106, 107

U

Ulster, 6, 18, 25, 31, 39, 75, 78
United Church (of Canada), 28
United Empire Loyalists, 15, 26, 51
United States (of America), 14, 26

V

Vimy Ridge, Battle of, 1917, 75, 115

W

War of 1812, 14, 15, 75, 114

CPSIA information can be obtained
at www.ICGtesting.com
Printed in the USA
LVOW13*1745301017
554317LV00013B/356/P